LEARN RIBBONCRAFT

Eve Harlow

COLLINS

First published in 1985
by William Collins Sons & Co Ltd
London · Glasgow · Sydney
Auckland · Johannesburg · Toronto

Reprinted 1986, 1989

© William Collins Sons & Co Ltd, 1985

Designed and edited by TL Creative Services
Illustrated by Hannah Hammond
Special photography by Di Lewis

ISBN 0 00 411932 0

Typeset by Wells Photoset
Printed by New Interlitho, Italy

Contents

Introduction

Ribboncraft is a new idea in needlecrafts. Until a few years ago the word 'ribboncraft' had no meaning. Traditional crafts using ribbon – such as ribbon weaving and Victorian ribbon embroidery – had almost disappeared and the techniques forgotton. Ribbons, it seemed, had been left behind in the 19th century.

In 1970, an American company, C.M. Offray & Son Inc, the world's largest manufacturer of woven ribbons, pioneered the development of polyester ribbons. With washable, colourfast, easy-care ribbons now available, a whole range of needlecrafts and techniques using ribbon became possible. Ribbons came into the 20th century.

In this book, you'll find the traditional crafts of ribbon weaving and ribbon embroidery, updated with modern materials. You'll also find some new ways with ribbon – patchwork and candlewicking, smocking and quilting – and the secrets of making beautiful ribbon roses.

All the things in this book were made with Offray ribbons and many of the designs were originated in Offray's Design Studio. This book would not have been possible without the help and assistance of the Offray organisation and they have our grateful thanks.

Ribbon Embroidery

One of the oldest ribboncraft techniques recorded is that of ribbon embroidery. Traditionally, ribbon embroidery is couched, flowers and leaves being formed by folding and pleating ribbons and catching down the edges. Modern ribbon embroidery introduces the use of simple surface stitches. Ribbon embroidery is essentially a freestyle form of decoration. The general outline of the design is indicated on the fabric with basting stitches or chalk pencil, and the work is carried out according to the creativity of the embroiderer.

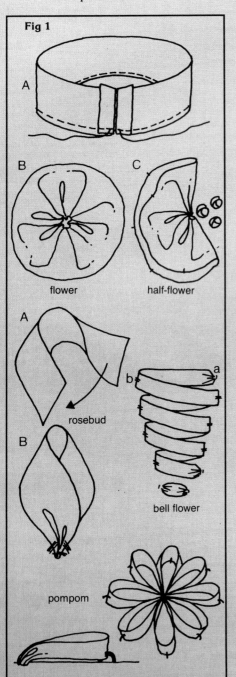

Fig 1

flower   half-flower

rosebud

bell flower

pompom

Victorian posy

The framed embroidery is worked on an oval shape 20×16cm (8×6½in).

Materials required

30×26cm (12×10¼in) pink fabric
1m (1⅛yd) double face polyester satin ribbons of each of the following: 1.5mm (1/16in)-wide Light Pink 117, Pink 150, Dusty Rose 160, Persimmon 240, Willow 563; 3mm (⅛in)-wide Rosy Mauve 165, Rose Pink 154, Willow 563; 10mm (⅜in)-wide Light Pink 117
1m (1⅛yd) of 10mm (⅜in)-wide Feather-edge satin ribbon in Peach 720, Light Pink 117
Anchor stranded embroidery threads in Cream 0386, Moss 0264, Geranium 541, Rose 048
Small crystal beads
Card, pelmet-weight interfacing, clear adhesive
Tapestry needle, embroidery needle

Working the design

To catch down the different kinds of ribbon flowers, use tiny, single stitches, which should be hidden under the ribbons. Always start with a back stitch on the wrong side and finish off stitches on the wrong side. Stitches may be worked from one ribbon flower to the next.

Using two strands of embroidery thread in the needle for stitching, work from the picture, adapting the placing of the various flowers, etc, to please your own sense of design. Remember that this is a freestyle technique and your own ideas should be expressed.

In ribbon embroidery, ribbon ends are caught to the back of the work with small hand-sewing stitches. Work with about 45cm (18in) of ribbon in the needle for surface stitches. If the ribbon twists, drop the needle and allow the ribbon to untwist.

Fig 1 illustrates a few of the shapes that can be achieved with ribbon. Surface stitches in Victorian Posy include Detached Chain, Open Chain and French Knots, some worked in narrow ribbons, some in stranded threads.

Finishing

Do not press ribbon embroidery. Cut card into shape to fit a frame. Cut stiff interfacing to the same shape and size. Lay the embroidery wrong side up and place the card on top. Pencil round lightly and trim the fabric back to 4cm (1½in) from the pencilled line. Lay embroidery wrong side up again and place interfacing, then card, on top. Bring the edges of the fabric on to the card and glue down, pulling the fabric smooth and ensuring that there are no creases or pleats on the right side of the work. Leave to dry, then place in a frame.

*Fig 1 **Flower:** join cut ends of ribbon and gather one edge (A). Draw up into a rosette (B)*
***Half-flower:** fold flower and couch down centre. Add a few French Knots (C)*
***Rosebud:** fold ribbon (A) and join cut ends, gathering and stitching down (B)*
***Bell flower:** bring ribbon through fabric at (a). Fold and catch it down at (b). Continue folding and catching down to make a bell shape. Take end back through fabric*
***Pompom:** fold and stitch ribbon into loops and catch down on selvedge edges of loops*

Designed by Mary Pilcher

Victorian dressmaker roses

Stitched ribbon roses, sometimes found in pieces of Victorian ribbon embroidery, also make a pretty trim. In the late 19th century, when ballgowns were full-skirted, girls made garlands of roses to go round the hems of their dresses, and trimmed bonnets with ribbon flowers.

You can use dressmaker roses on all kinds of fashion clothes, knitwear, children's and babies' clothes, and they are particularly decorative on summery hats and for brides' accessories. Polyester satin ribbons are ideal for making ribbon roses, as they are both colourfast and washable.

Dressmaker roses also make a very charming touch on soft furnishings – for bedcovers, on curtain tie-backs, stitched to scatter cushions and pillows and on room accessories, such as soft boxes, tidies and picture frames. You will find examples of stitched ribbon roses used in this way throughout the book. The pretty soft boxes and picture frame on page 1 are decorated with ribbon roses, and all the items illustrated were made from Simplicity Pattern No. 5743.

When choosing ribbons for rose-making, the width of the ribbon determines the size of the finished rose. Wide ribbons make full-blown cabbage roses for hats; narrow ribbons make small roses for lingerie and babies' clothes. Depending upon the fullness of the rose you want, 1m *(approx 1yd)* of ribbon will make two to three roses.

Materials required

Single face polyester satin ribbon
Matching Drima sewing threads

Basic techniques

1. Thread the needle, knot the thread end. Roll the ribbon end into a tight tube, about three turns. Make two or three stitches to hold the bottom of the tube (Fig 1). This is the 'bud'.
2. Put the needle down, leaving thread attached. Fold ribbon end diagonally away from you (Fig 2). Moving only your right hand, turn the 'bud' on to the fold, centring it (Fig 3). Continue turning the bud on to the fold in the ribbon until the ribbon is straight again (Fig 4). Now make two or three small stitches at the base of the rose.
3. To make the petals fold the ribbon away from you diagonally again and move the bud (now a cone shape) on to the fold. Keep the rose open in shape. Stitch each petal as you make it (Fig 5).
4. Make as many petals as you require. Cut the ribbon off square and bring the end down to the base of the rose. Gather the cut edge, finishing off the stitches securely (Fig 6). Use the thread to sew the rose to the fabric as required.

Rose-trimmed hats

Pink hat

Make three Silver 012 and two White 029 roses from 39mm *(1½in)*-wide ribbon. Make two White 029 roses from 23mm *(⅞in)*-wide ribbon. Tie 1m *(1⅛yd)* of 7mm *(¼in)*-wide Silver 012 ribbon at front. Cut off ends. Stitch roses as illustrated through the straw. Sew loops of Silver ribbon between roses.

Blue hat

Make five roses from 39mm *(1½in)*-wide Navy 370 ribbon. Make four roses from 23mm *(⅞in)*-wide Navy 370 ribbon. Sew roses to hat front. From 2m *(2¼yd)* of 3mm *(⅛in)*-wide white spotted Navy 370 ribbon make loops and sew between roses.

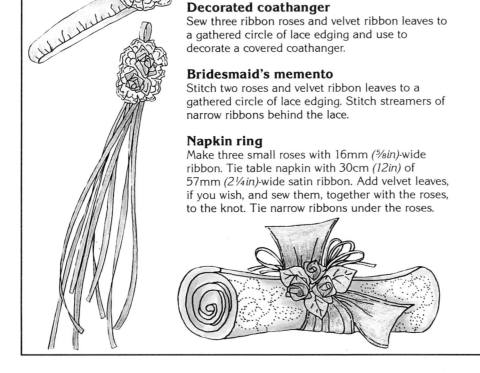

Quick makes with dressmaker roses

Decorated coathanger

Sew three ribbon roses and velvet ribbon leaves to a gathered circle of lace edging and use to decorate a covered coathanger.

Bridesmaid's memento

Stitch two roses and velvet ribbon leaves to a gathered circle of lace edging. Stitch streamers of narrow ribbons behind the lace.

Napkin ring

Make three small roses with 16mm *(⅝in)*-wide ribbon. Tie table napkin with 30cm *(12in)* of 57mm *(2¼in)*-wide satin ribbon. Add velvet leaves, if you wish, and sew them, together with the roses, to the knot. Tie narrow ribbons under the roses.

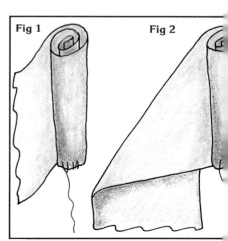

Fig 1   Fig 2

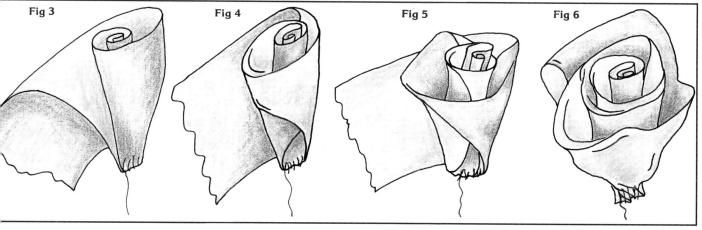

Fig 3

Fig 4

Fig 5

Fig 6

Summer daisies

Narrow ribbons can be used in place of conventional embroidery threads if the design and stitches are simple. The Summer Daisies design uses only three stitches: French Knots, Open Fishbone, and Lazy Daisy worked so that the point of the stitch lies on the outside edge of the finished flower.

Materials required

Finished size 43cm (17in) diameter
1.10m *(1¼yd)* of 114cm *(45in)*-wide
    blue polyester satin fabric
Matching Drima sewing thread
3.60m *(4yd)* piping cord
1.5mm *(¹⁄₁₆in)*-wide double face
    polyester satin ribbons as follows:
    5m *(5½yd)* Mint 530; 3m *(3¼yd)*
    Light Pink 117, Light Orchid 430,
    Light Blue 305; 3.50m *(3⅞yd)* Iris
    447
Tissue paper, basting thread

Preparation

From the fabric, cut a circle 30cm *(12in)* diameter for the embroidery. For the cushion cut two circles 45cm *(18in)* diameter. From one circle cut a round hole in the middle 19cm *(7½in)* diameter. From the remaining blue fabric cut and join 10cm *(4in)*-wide strips to make a 1.45m *(1⅝yd)* length for the gusset. Cut bias strips 2.5cm *(1in)* wide to cover the piping cord. Cut the cord into two pieces, 1.45m *(1⅝yd)* and 67cm *(26½in)* long, and cover with bias strips.

Place the 30cm *(12in)* fabric circle in an embroidery frame. Trace the lines of the design from the facing page on to tissue paper. Baste tissue to the fabric.

Working the design

Work embroidery through the tissue paper and follow the picture for colours and stitches.

Stems are ribbon couched down with ribbon (Fig 1). Petals and leaves are worked in reversed Lazy Daisy stitches (Fig 2). French Knots are worked for flower centres and Open Fishbone for grass heads.

When embroidery is completed, gently tear away the tissue and remove embroidery from the frame.

Cut the circle of fabric back to 24cm *(9½in)* in diameter.

Making up the cushion

On the cushion piece with the hole, pin, baste and machine-stitch the covered piping round the hole edge on the right side, cut edge of fabric to cut edge. Press seam allowance to the wrong side. Place the embroidery underneath and baste in place. Stitch from the wrong side, working stitches along previous row of piping stitching.

Pin, baste and stitch piping round the outside edge of the same cushion piece. Pin, baste and stitch piping round the edge of the second cushion piece on the right side.

Pin the short ends of the gusset piece and check that it fits round the cushion. Baste and stitch short ends. Pin, baste and stitch the gusset to the top cushion piece, right sides facing. Work the second cushion piece to the gusset in the same way, leaving a 25cm *(10in)* gap in the seam for inserting the cushion pad. Close seam with hand-sewing.

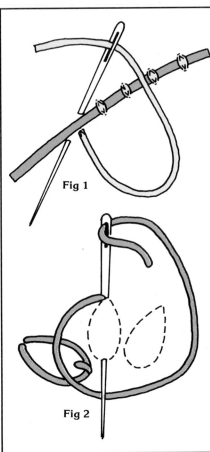

Fig 1

Fig 2

Fig 1 *Couching for stems*

Fig 2 *Reversed Lazy Daisy for petals and leaves*

Delicate summer colours in ribbon embroidery worked on polyester satin make a pretty cushion. Above, the panel is reproduced life-size for you to trace

Little town

In traditional ribbon embroidery, techniques tend to produce flower and foliage effects. Here is an example of modern ribbon embroidery where narrow ribbons have been couched down on fabric in rows to produce solid areas of colour. In some places, Straight stitches have been used for couching; in others, Cross stitches produce a more textured effect. Other decorative surface embroidery stitches may be used to couch ribbons for an even greater variety of effects.

The stitch guide and key are shown overleaf.

Materials required

Finished size 24×26cm (9½×10¼in)
50×56cm *(20×22in)* cream even-weave linen or similar fabric
24×26cm *(9½×10¼in)* stitch-and-tear embroidery backing material
1.5mm *(¹⁄₁₆ in)*-wide double face polyester satin ribbons as follows: 7.50m *(8¼yd)* Light Blue 305; 6m *(6⅝yd)* Silver 012, Pink 150; 4.50m *(5yd)* White 029; 3.50m *(3⅞yd)* Baby Maize 617; 2.50m *(2¾yd)* Red 250, Emerald 580, Tan 835; 2m *(2¼yd)* Sable 843, Capri Blue 337; 1.60m *(1¾yd)* Persimmon 240, Peach 720, Strawberry 157, Hot Pink 156, Sienna 770; 1m *(1⅛yd)* Lemon 640, Turftan 847, Rosewood 169, Willow 563, Light Orchid 430
Anchor stranded embroidery threads as follows: 1 skein of Emerald 0227, Terra Cotta 0336, Grey 0397; oddments of Forest Green 0218, Grass Green 0242, Peat 0360, Beige 0379, Terra Cotta 0341, Nasturtium 0328, Cobalt Blue 0131, 0128, Kingfisher 0160, Canary 0288, Gorse 0300, Blossom Pink 038, Rose 048, Old Rose 076, Red 047, White 0402, Black 0403
Tissue paper, basting thread
Matching Drima sewing threads

Preparation

Trace your pattern from the stitch guide overleaf. Use a ruler to outline the houses, then draw in the flowers, trees, path, flower beds, clock face and round-topped doors, etc.

Press all creases from the fabric.

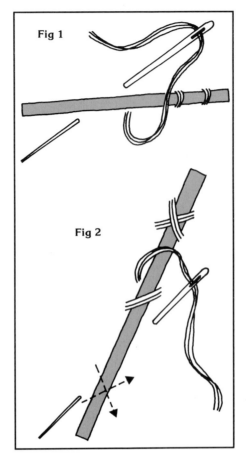

Fig 1 *Couching down ribbon with Straight stitches in embroidery thread*

Fig 2 *Couching down ribbon with Cross stitches in embroidery thread*

Mark the centre of the fabric with threads and then measure and mark the working area 24×26cm *(9½×10¼in)* from the centre, in threads. Baste the stitch-and-tear material to the back of the fabric on the working area. Pin the traced pattern to the fabric and work small running stitches along all the pattern lines. When completed, gently tear away the tissue paper. Put the fabric in an embroidery frame.

Basic techniques for working with ribbons and threads

1. Cut ribbons into approximately 45cm *(18in)* lengths. Use three strands of embroidery threads together throughout the work. Follow the stitch guide overleaf for the direction of couching and as a guide to the use of Straight stitch and Cross stitch.

2. Thread a length of ribbon into a large-eyed but sharp needle and

Designed by Linda Wood

bring it through from the wrong side of the fabric, leaving about 2cm (¾in) at the back. Catch down the end with a few hand-sewing stitches.

3. To couch with Straight stitches, see previous page, Fig 1. Bring the embroidery thread through from the wrong side and, laying the ribbon with the thumb, make the first stitch to hold the ribbon in position, taking the needle through to the wrong side. Bring the needle through again a short distance away (see Fig 1) for the second couching stitch.

4. To couch with Cross stitches, see previous page, Fig 2.

5. When you reach the end of the first row of couching take the ribbon on its needle under three or four threads of fabric and bring it through to the front again ready for the second row. As you can see from the picture of the Little Town on the previous page, couching stitches are alternated between those of the previous row, to simulate bricks or roof tiles.

6. To finish a length of ribbon, take the end through to the wrong side and secure with hand-sewing stitches.

7. Complete all the ribbon work first,

then work the freestyle decorative embroidery using stranded threads. Do not press ribbonwork because it spoils the effect.

Working the design

The stitch guide shows the direction in which the ribbon is laid and where Straight stitches and Cross stitches are used for couching. The key below identifies ribbon colours and embroidery threads for each area of the picture. Refer to the picture on the previous page for the embroidery stitches used for flowers, foliage, sky, path, etc.

Work paths, lawns and sky in Seeding. Flowers are worked in French Knots, Open Chain stitch, Straight stitch and Lazy Daisy. Outline windows and doors in Stem stitch. The church door looks very effective outlined with a flat plait (see page 23, Fig 1) of Silver 012 ribbon. Use stranded threads for smaller leaves, branches and flower stems.

Right, stitch guide for the Little Town picture on the previous page, showing directional working for couching down ribbons

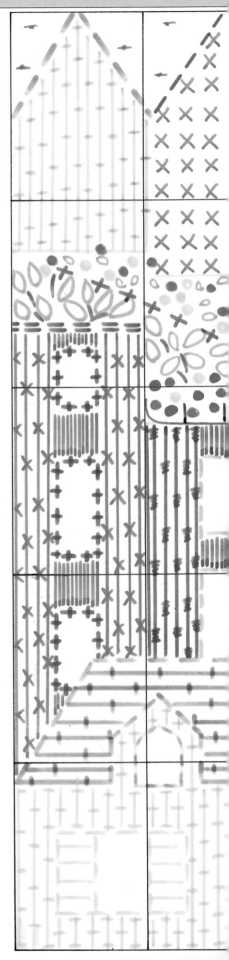

Key to stitch guide

Ribbons	(couched with) Threads
Silver 012	Grey 0397
White 029	Grey 0397
White 029	White 0402
Baby Maize 617	Gorse 0300
Peach 720	Peat 0360
Persimmon 240	Nasturtium 0328
Pink 150	Rose 048
Rosewood 169	Old Rose 076
Light Blue 305	Kingfisher 0160
Capri Blue 337	Cobalt Blue 0131
Sable 843	Beige 0379
Turftan 847	Peat 0360
Tan 835	Peat 0360
Sienna 770	
Light Blue 305	
Silver 012	

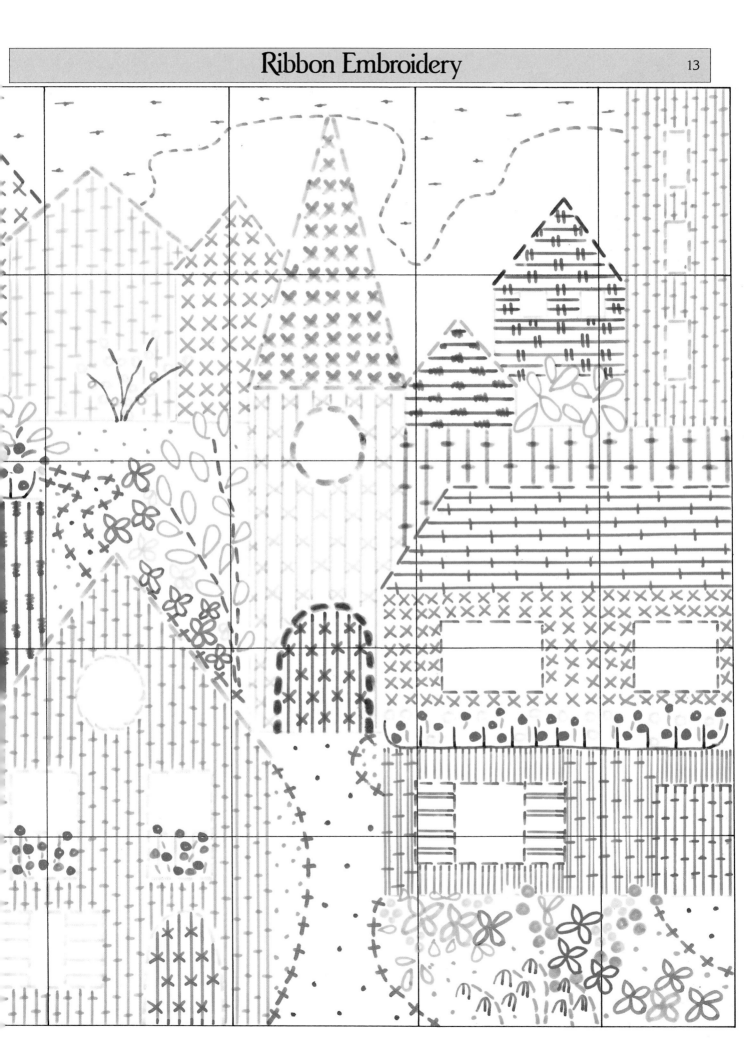

Hanging planter

The pretty planter is made of plastic canvas embroidered with ribbons. Florentine or Bargello stitch has been used here but any straight stitch with a similar effect could be used. Plastic canvas, a comparatively new embroidery material, is useful when a strong structure is being worked, such as a picture frame or a box. Plastic canvas is also ideal for making church kneelers, book covers, purses and bags – as well as fashion accessories and soft jewellery.

Ribbons work well on this material used either with tapisserie yarns for textural interest or, as on the planter, when a hard-wearing finish is required. As polyester ribbons are washable and colourfast, the embroidered planter can be washed if it becomes soiled and the colours will not fade in strong sunlight.

Materials required

Finished size 12.5×11.5cm (5×4½in)
Sheet of plastic canvas 7 holes to
    2.5cm *(1in)*
3mm *(⅛in)*-wide double face
    polyester satin ribbons as follows:
    8.25m *(9yd)* Indian Orange 756;
    8.25m *(9yd)* Yellow Gold 660;
    33m *(36yd)* Cream 815
2.50m *(2¾yd)* white cotton
    furnishing cord and a tassel
2 pieces of 11.5cm *(4½in)* square
    stiff card
Tapestry needle, hand-sewing needle
White Drima sewing thread

Preparation

Cut four pieces of plastic canvas 12.5×11.5cm *(5×4½in)* for the sides of the planter, making sure that the edges are cut smooth.

Cut a piece of plastic canvas 11.5cm *(4½in)* square for the planter base.

Working the design

Follow the picture as a guide to ribbon colours and the chart (Fig 1) for the stitchery, which shows one repeat. Each panel is worked with two and a half repeats, making five 'flame' points.

The chart shows the sequence of stitches from the foundation in

Indian Orange to the completion of the rows in Yellow Gold. When you have worked the last row of Yellow Gold the stitchery continues with Cream ribbon over four threads of canvas.

Row 1: Using Indian Orange ribbon in the needle and starting at the left, work the first stitch over two threads of canvas, the next stitch over four, then alternate over two, over four to the end of the row. The last stitch, on the right, is over four threads.

Row 2: In this row, the 'flame' points are established, which will enable you to work the remainder of the Florentine pattern. Still using Indian Orange ribbon and working from right to left, make the first stitch over the last but one stitch of the previous row and over four threads of canvas. Work two more stitches and you will see that you have completed your first 'flame' point. Now miss the next three stitches of the previous row and begin the second flame point on the fourth stitch. Continue in the same way right across the row, stepping stitches up and down in a zigzag pattern.

Row 3: Change to the Yellow Gold ribbon. You now have the basis of the pattern in Indian Orange to follow. Work from left to right and over four threads of canvas, placing each stitch immediately over each of the Indian Orange stitches.

Row 4: Work from right to left in Yellow Gold as you did for row 3.

Change to Cream ribbon and work the panel until you are within five threads of the edge. Complete the panel by working in Cream over five and three threads alternately.

Work all four side panels of the planter in the same way.

Working the base

Use Cream ribbon throughout for the base. Work the first row exactly as for the sides, then continue working over four threads of canvas. The last row is worked over six and four threads alternately.

Finishing

Using Cream ribbon, oversew one side piece to the base piece, working from the right side and working each stitch through one hole of canvas on the edges. Sew the second side piece

to the base, then the third and finally the fourth. Now work oversewing stitches to join the corners of the planter, still working from the right side.

Press the two pieces of stiff card into the base of the planter. Work oversewing stitches with Cream ribbon all round the top edge of the planter. To neaten the inside, hand-sew a small white plastic bag just inside the top edge, taking small stitches through the plastic canvas.

Hanging the planter

Cut the cotton cord into two pieces. Wind cotton round the cut ends and sew to prevent the cord fraying. Pin the cord on to the bottom of the planter in a cross and then take the four ends up the side seams. Stitch the cord to the planter with hand-sewing stitches and thread. Knot the four ends at the top for hanging. (Slip a large brass ring on to the knot if preferred.) Sew the tassel underneath the planter.

Fig 1 *Stitch chart for the Hanging Planter, showing one repeat and the sequence of stitches from the foundation in Indian Orange to the completion of the rows in Yellow Gold*

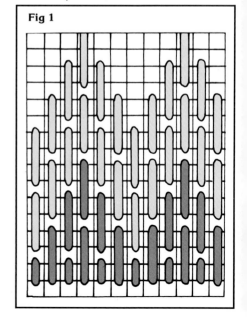

Fig 1

Hints on working ribbons on plastic canvas

Do not knot the ribbon end when starting embroidery. Hold the end down on the wrong side with your thumb and work the first two or three stitches over the end to secure it. When finishing a length of ribbon, work the end under previous stitches.

Ribbon tends to twist while working but this can be minimised if you hold the ribbon smooth and flat along the canvas as you make each stitch. Slip the needle through, holding the ribbon down firmly on the canvas with the thumb. Pull the ribbon through and the stitch will remain smooth on the right side. Do the same as you prepare to bring the ribbon back through from the wrong side. Hold the ribbon smoothly with the fingers against the canvas on the wrong side and as you bring the needle through, keep your fingers in position, holding the ribbon.

You will get a little twisting even using this technique but small twists are easily removed with the needle point. If the ribbon should twist excessively, drop the needle and allow the ribbon to untwist naturally.

More ideas for plastic canvas

Plastic canvas can also be obtained in a finer mesh of 10 holes to 2.5cm (1in), and 1.5mm (1/16 in)-wide ribbon can be used on this. This finer-mesh plastic canvas is ideal for making bracelets, hairbands, bookmarks and soft jewellery. Bracelets are made with plastic canvas strips 25cm (10in) long by 2.5cm (1in) wide. Leave 12mm (1/2 in) unworked at one end and overlap the ends. Embroider and oversew edges to finish through both thicknesses of canvas.

Hairbands worked in ribbons on plastic canvas look pretty and fashionable. Cut plastic canvas to about the same length as for bracelets but a little wider. Leave two holes of plastic canvas unworked at the ends, snip the plastic threads with scissors and slip elastic through the holes to fasten the hairband.

For bookmarks, which make very pretty gifts, embroider strips of fine-mesh plastic canvas, and soft jewellery, such as brooches, earrings and pendants, is particularly effective worked with Lurex ribbons.

Candlewicking with ribbon

Candlewicking is a traditional American craft dating back to pioneer days when women used the linen yarn intended for candle wicks to embroider coarse, unbleached linen, in an attempt to make their home furnishings more attractive. The same simple stitches, worked in narrow, cream ribbons on natural-coloured fabrics, are a modern interpretation of an old and charming craft.

Butterfly motif

The butterfly design is worked on even-weave cotton and, on this fabric, could be mounted and framed for a wall picture. As the butterfly is such a versatile motif, however, it could also be worked as a decoration for fashion accessories or home furnishings (see illustrations).

Fig 1 Trace the butterfly, then reverse the tracing to obtain the whole motif

Materials required

Finished motif size 11×20cm (4½ × 8in)
12m *(13¼yd)* of 1.5mm *(¹⁄₁₆ in)*-wide Cream 815 double face polyester satin ribbon
40×33cm *(16×13in)* unbleached cotton fabric
1 ball of Pearl cotton, Ecru No 5
Tissue paper, basting thread

Preparation

Trace the butterfly motif from Fig 1 and reverse the tracing to obtain the whole motif. Put the fabric into an embroidery frame. Baste the tracing to the fabric, or use dressmakers' carbon paper.

Working the design

Work stitches through the tissue paper, if you are using this technique, tearing the paper away when embroidery is completed.
Work the design as follows:
Head and tail: Straight Satin stitch in ribbon.
Body of butterfly: Slanting Satin stitch in Pearl cotton, outlined with Stem stitch in Pearl cotton.

Antenna and oval shapes on the wings: Palestrina stitch (Fig 2) in Pearl cotton.
Black dots: Colonial Knots (Fig 3) in ribbon.
Crosses: Colonial Knots in Pearl cotton.
Flower petals: Lazy Daisy stitches in ribbon first, then work a second petal on top in Pearl cotton.

Finishing

It is advisable not to press ribbon embroidery but if it is really necessary, press lightly with the embroidery face down on a towel.

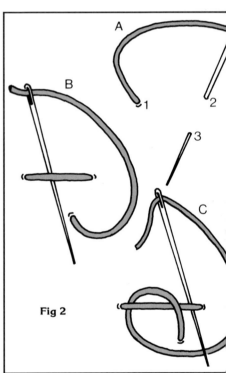

Fig 2 Palestrina stitch: this is worked from left to right. Bring needle up through fabric (A1). Make a stitch to the right about 6mm (¼in) away (A2) and come up through the fabric about 3mm (⅛in) below and slightly to the left (A3). Pull the thread through, then go back over and under the straight stitch (B). Without tightening the thread, again go under the straight stitch (C). Now pull the thread through gently to form the stitch. Make the next stitch to the right by inserting the needle 6mm (¼in) away, as A1-2

Fig 3 Colonial Knot: bring needle through to right side of fabric at A1 and swing thread around needle in a clockwise loop. Wrap the thread anticlockwise around the needle in a figure-of-eight (B). Pull thread around needle gently and reinsert the needle a few threads away from the point the stitch was first started (Fig A1). Pull thread through fabric to make the Colonial Knot. Bring thread up through fabric again to the right side to make the next Knot

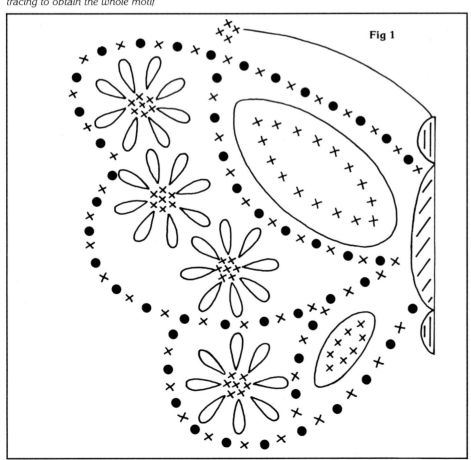

Fig 1

Above, the butterfly motif is 11×20cm (4½×8in) and is worked here on cream even-weave cotton for a mounted and framed picture

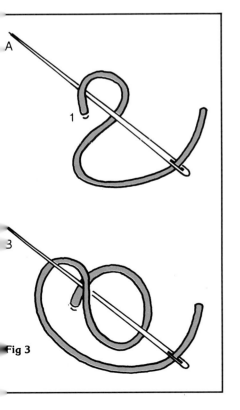

Fig 3

Ideas for the butterfly motif

Candlewicking, using a few simple stitches, Pearl cotton and narrow ribbon, can be used to decorate all kinds of home furnishings and accessories. Use the butterfly motif for a cushion or pillow, working in white on a pastel-coloured fabric and edging the cushion with broderie anglaise (eyelet). Or work butterflies along the hem of curtains for a pretty bedroom scheme, with perhaps a single butterfly worked on a runner.

For personal items, the butterfly might be embroidered on even-weave linen for a wooden-handled work bag or, for a charming fashion look, on the back of a casual summer linen jacket.

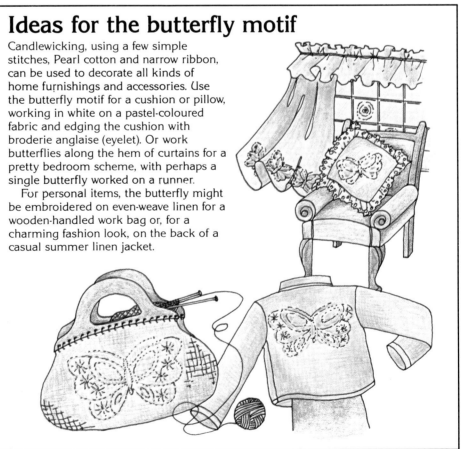

Smocking

Smocking with fine ribbon lends a whole new dimension to the needlecraft. Bold and colourful effects can be achieved and fabrics such as furnishing cottons and wools can be worked. This means that ribbon smocking can be used not only for dresses, shirts, aprons and so on, but also for furnishings for the home.

Fabrics for smocking

Suitable fabrics for ribbon smocking are cotton and cotton mixes, linen-type fabrics, fine wools and some furnishing fabrics. Very thick fabrics do not look so well when smocked. Traditionally, transfers of smocking dots are used as a guide to gathering the pleats, but if you are using fabric with a recognisable repeat or overall pattern, such as spots or gingham checks, you can dispense with the transfer and use the pattern itself as your guide.

Smocking reduces fabric to one-third of its original width and you should allow for this when measuring and buying fabric.

Stitches in smocking

Three stitches only are all you need for ribbon smocking. Stem stitch, sometimes called Outline stitch (Fig 1), is used for firm control of gathers and is thus used at the top of a smocked band. Cable stitch (Fig 2) is used for medium control. Surface Honeycomb (Figs 3A and B) is a looser control stitch and, used at the bottom of a band, will release the fullness. The curtain heading in the picture is worked entirely in rows of Surface Honeycomb.

Smocked curtains

Materials required

For a pair of curtains with a finished hem width of 152cm (60in) × 91cm (36in) long

3.50m (4yd) of 120cm (48in)-wide printed cotton fabric

4m (4½yd) of 1.5mm (¹⁄₁₆ in)-wide Red 250 double face polyester satin ribbon

Curtain hooks or rings as required

Preparation

Cut and seam the fabric to make two pieces 155cm (61in) wide by 107cm (42in) long. Press seams open and neaten edges.

Turn the top edge of curtain over 5cm (2in) and press. The first row of gathering stitches is worked through the doubled fabric, 4cm (1½in) from the top edge. Work six rows of gathering stitches from side edge to side edge, the rows 15mm (⅝in) apart. Gathering stitches should also be about 15mm (⅝in) apart for this project. (They can be as close as 6mm (¼in), depending on the fabric and the design.)

Pull up the six rows of gathering and twist the thread ends in pairs around pins (Fig 4). The width of the work should now be approximately 55cm (22in). Adjust the pleats evenly. In smocking, the pleats are called 'reeds'.

Follow Figs 3A and B to work Surface Honeycomb, using ribbon in the needle. Ribbon ends should be fastened off on the wrong side of work for starting and finishing lengths; use small hand-stitches to catch ribbon to the fabric.

Finishing

When all smocking has been completed, carefully withdraw the gathering threads. Do not press smocking.

To make up the curtains make narrow hems on both edges and machine-stitch. Press the hem fold to desired length. Machine-stitch a single narrow fold on the edge, then hand-sew the hem. Sew curtain hooks or rings to curtain head behind the smocking.

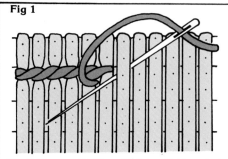

Fig 1 *Stem* or *Outline stitch* is a tight control stitch. Work from left to right along lines of gathering. Pick up one reed (pleat) with each stitch. Stem stitch can be varied by stepping stitches between rows to make patterns

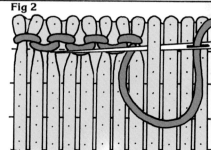

Fig 2 *Cable stitch* is a medium control stitch and each stitch joins two reeds. Work from left to right with the thread placed above and below the needle alternately. Several rows of Cable stitches can be worked close together

Worked by Cathryn Brooker

Smocking ideas

Lampshade and base

The lampshade cover is smocked on the top edge with Stem stitch and Surface Honeycomb. The smocked cover for the base is worked with rows of Stem stitch and Cable stitch at the neck, with looser Surface Honeycomb stitches lower down.

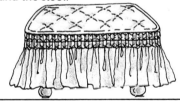

Tablecloth

A circle of fabric is cut to fit the table top, then a straight length is smocked on the top edge to fit round the circle.

Footstool

The top piece is quilted fabric, which is stitched to a straight piece of fabric smocked along the top edge to fit round the stool.

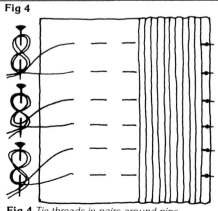

Fig 3A

Fig 3A *Surface Honeycomb is worked over two rows of gathers. Take thread over two reeds in the top row and bring needle out at the side of the second reed. The thread lies on the surface while the needle moves down to the lower row*

Fig 3B

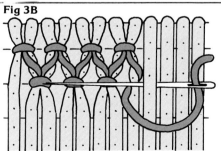

Fig 3B *Take needle back through the second reed in the lower row and then over to the third reed, pulling reeds two and three together. The thread then lies on the third reed while the needle moves up to the top row again*

Fig 4

Fig 4 *Tie threads in pairs around pins*

Ribbon Appliqué

Appliqué is the term used for applying a small piece of fabric to a larger piece, but when the term is used for ribbon a whole range of new ideas and techniques becomes possible. Once you begin to think of ribbon as a narrow fabric with two edges already finished off for you, ribbon becomes the simplest material to use for decoratively banding garments and house furnishings.

Developing the idea, ribbon need not be stitched down on both edges — it can be left partially free of the background fabric. The finished edges also mean that embroidery stitches can be used to apply ribbons — by hand or by machine — and this leads to ideas about couching ribbons. At this point, the enthusiastic needlewoman has evolved ideas for gathering, pleating, twisting, knotting, plaiting and shirring ribbon and applying it to background fabric in dozens of ways. The ribbon appliqué samplers on pages 22-23 show just a few ways in which ribbon can be used for applied decorative effects.

Types of ribbons

Only polyester ribbons should be used for appliqué if the finished item is to be washed or dry-cleaned.

Ribbons are available in a vast range of colours, textures and patternings. Satins and grosgrains can be plain or woven into stripes and Jacquards. Ribbons come printed with spots or with decorative motifs such as flowers, hearts, stars, ships, whales and anchors — or with familiar characters such as Snoopy and Woodstock. Jacquard ribbons can be prettily floral or brilliant and striking with touches of glitter. Lurex ribbons in silver, gold, pewter and copper provide opportunities for dramatic effects, while polyester velvet ribbons add a luxurious dimension to appliqué designs.

Working with ribbons

Although reputable brands of polyester ribbons are washable, it is always advisable to launder both ribbons and the background fabric before using them for appliqué.

Ribbons should be basted rather than pinned in position, working basting along both selvedges because once pinholes are made in ribbon it is virtually impossible to remove them.

Ribbons can be stitched down by hand or by machine, using straight, zigzag or embroidery stitches. Using straight machine stitches, always work in the same direction on both edges to minimise puckering. A commercial bonding material is available which makes ribbon appliqué very easy. It is made in four ribbon widths and is simply laid along placement lines, the ribbon positioned on top and then ironed on to the fabric. The ribbon adheres smoothly and machine-stitching can then be worked without basting. Polyester ribbons should not require pressing after appliqué but if it is necessary, make sure that all basting threads (and pins) are removed first.

Ribbons, lace and broderie (eyelet) used together give a rich but fresh feeling in bedroom furnishings. The tucked bedcover is made from white sheeting, with a deep broderie (eyelet) frill trimmed with ribbon-threaded lace and piped with polyester satin ribbon. Matching pillows have wide frills appliquéd with narrow ribbon. This pretty scheme could be developed with a broderie (eyelet)-covered lampshade trimmed with dressmaker roses (see page 40) or with a ribbon-woven nightdress case, using White 029 and Mint 530 polyester satin ribbons (see instructions for ribbon weaving on pages 46-49)

Photograph: Pins and Needles Magazine

Appliqué samplers

Here are just a few of the dozens of ways in which ribbon can be applied to fabric to produce colourful or pretty effects. Try each of them as a sampler for your own library of appliqué ideas — and others are sure to occur to you.

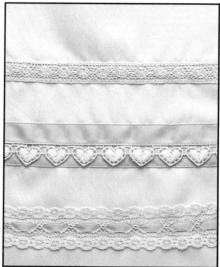

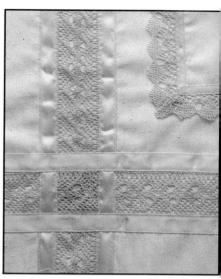

Top left: 23mm *(⅞in)*-wide satin ribbon is pleated and stitched to the ground fabric. 7mm *(¼in)*-wide ribbon is overlaid down the middle and stitched on both edges to hold pleats to fabric. The appliqué band is then pressed.

Centre: 23mm *(⅞in)*-wide satin ribbon is gathered on one edge and stitched to the ground fabric. 7mm *(¼in)*-wide ribbon is laid along the gathers and stitched on both edges.

Bottom right: pleated 23mm *(⅞in)*-wide satin ribbon is stitched to fabric through a flat plait of 1.5mm *(1⁄16 in)*-wide ribbon (Fig 1).

Top row: 13mm *(½in)*-wide lace is overlaid on satin ribbon of the same width and stitched along both edges of the lace through the ribbon to the ground fabric.

Centre row: 13mm *(½in)*-wide satin ribbon is stitched on both edges and guipure lace is laid over it. A second piece of ribbon is placed above the first and over the straight edge of the lace. It is then stitched down.

Bottom row: eyelet or beading lace is threaded with ribbon and stitched to the ground fabric.

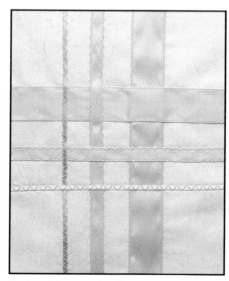

Satin ribbons of different widths are laid and interwoven, each ribbon being stitched as it is applied. Wide ribbons are stitched with straight stitches, medium-width ribbons with zigzag machine-stitch. Very narrow ribbons are couched down with zigzag stitches.

Textured interest is achieved with thick cotton lace and satin ribbons. 3cm *(1¼in)*-wide lace is set in a cross. 13mm *(½in)*-wide ribbon is laid over lace vertically and stitched on both edges, then horizontally and stitched.

Above right: 7mm *(¼in)*-wide ribbon is appliquéd along straight edge of lace trim.

Top left and bottom right: triangles of satin ribbon are folded and pressed (as turquoise sample), then basted to the ground fabric. A strip of ribbon is laid on the edge of the triangles and stitched on both edges to the ground fabric.

Centre: regular zigzag folds in satin ribbon are pressed, then basted to the ground fabric. A strip of ribbon of the same width is stitched over the bottom edge of the zigzag strip.

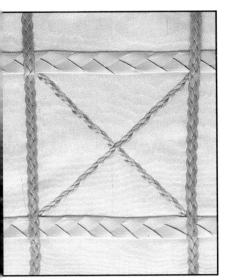

Three pieces of 10mm (3/8in)-wide pink satin ribbon are fold-plaited (Fig 2) and hand-sewn to the ground fabric. The lilac and multi-coloured satin ribbons are flat-plaited (Fig 1) and hand-sewn to the ground fabric.

Top row: a bow of flat-plaited 3mm (1/8in)-wide grosgrain ribbon is stitched to a hand-applied band of flat plait (Fig 1).
Centre row: a stitched satin ribbon bow is hand-sewn to a machine-applied ribbon of the same width.
Bottom row: a simple loop bow of 7mm (1/4in)-wide grosgrain ribbon is hand-sewn to an applied strip of the same width.

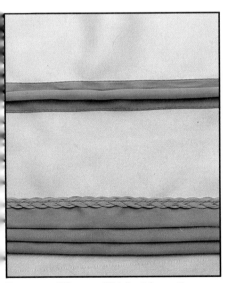

Top row: 23mm (7/8in)-wide satin ribbon is folded lengthwise. The fold is machine-stitched and pressed. The ribbon is then machine-stitched on both edges to the ground fabric and pressed flat.
Bottom row: three pieces of 23mm (7/8in)-wide satin ribbon are folded lengthwise and the fold pressed. The three pieces are laid with folds overlapping and each machine-stitched on the top edge to the ground fabric. A flat plait (Fig 1) trims the top row.

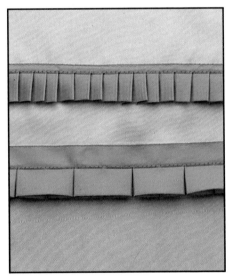

Top row: 23mm (7/8in)-wide satin ribbon is knife-pleated, basted to the ground fabric and pressed. 7mm (1/4in)-wide ribbon is stitched along the top edge.
Bottom row: box pleats are pressed into 23mm (7/8in)-wide satin ribbon and basted to the ground fabric. 16mm (5/8in)-wide ribbon is stitched along the top edge.

Ribbon plaits or braids

Plaited or braided ribbon is a very pretty form of ribbon appliqué. It can be machine- or hand-stitched, depending on the effect required, and can be worked in single or massed rows.

As a ribbon plait is flexible, it can be used where ordinary ribbon appliqué would be impossible, such as on the hem of a circular skirt or round a collar. Ribbon plaits make very good ties for belts and strong, yet pretty, straps for bags and purses. They also make non-slip straps for lingerie.

Two different plaits are possible with ribbons, the flat plait and the folded plait. The flat plait can be worked only with 1.5mm and 3mm (1/16 in and 1/8in)-wide ribbon. The folded technique can be worked on ribbon up to 13mm (1/2in) wide.

Fig 1 shows how the flat plait is worked. The ribbons are brought forward without folding. Fig 2 shows the folded plait where ribbons are folded forward at each stage of the plaiting. Allow one-third more ribbon than the required finished length of the plait and pin all three ribbons together to a board or table top to plait.

Ribbon plaits should be pressed when they are completed.

Fig 1

Fig 2

Scatter cushions

Each of the cushions is designed to make effective use of ribbons of different widths. Many ribbon colours – subtle pale tints, fresh, bright colours and rich, dark shades – can be obtained as wide as 77mm (3in) through a range of sizes to a narrow 1.5mm (1/16 in). This enables the creative needlewoman to work with wide ribbons as though they were

Making cushion covers the easy way

Making cushion covers is simple if you use a 'pillow opening' instead of a zip fastener. The technique can be used on cushions and pillows of any shape and can also be adapted to duvet covers.

Cut the back of the cushion cover to the same depth as the front but 10cm (4in) wider. Cut the piece in two from top to bottom. Press a narrow fold to the wrong side on these cut edges. Fold again to make a 2.5cm (1in) hem. Stitch. Lay the two pieces together, overlapping the hemmed edges so that the cushion back is now the same width as the cushion front. Baste them together all round, right sides facing, then stitch. Turn to right side through the opening. The opening can be fastened with a button and thread loop, snap fasteners or ribbon ties.

Frilled edges

Applying a frilled or lace edge is easier when following the pillow opening method for a cushion cover. Gather the straight edge of the frill and fit it round the front cushion piece, allowing a little extra fullness at the corners. Join the short ends.

Pin and baste the gathered frill to the right side of the cushion front, arranging it so that the join is at a corner. The straight edge of the frill should lie along the edge of the cushion.

Lay the prepared cushion back on top, right side down. Baste all round, then stitch. Turn the cushion cover to the right side through the back opening.

Designed by Alison Palmer

pieces of fabric and then trim her work with the same colours in narrow ribbons. The Blue Balloons and the Cream and Mint cushions show the scope of ribbon appliqué.

Blue balloons

Materials required

Finished size 30cm (12in) square

2 pieces of 33cm (13in) square white polyester satin fabric

1.60m (1¾yd) of 10cm (4in)-wide white broderie anglaise (eyelet) edging

Copen Blue 335 single face polyester satin ribbons as follows: 20cm (8in) of 77mm (3in)-wide; 80cm (31in) of 16mm (⅝in)-wide; 1.40m (1½yd) of 7mm (¼in)-wide

30cm (12in) square cushion pad

Scraps of polyester wadding

Matching Drima sewing threads

Preparation

On thin card draw a rectangle 68mm (2⅝in) deep by 55mm (2⅛in) wide. Round off between the lines to make an oval shape to these dimensions. Cut out the oval for a template for the balloon shapes. Trace three balloons on to the wide Copen Blue 335 ribbon, about 1cm (⅜in) apart. Machine-stitch round the outlines with a narrow zigzag stitch. Cut out the three shapes with about 3mm (⅛in) allowance all round.

Position the balloons (as shown in the picture) on a square of white satin fabric. Baste in position, using a fine needle and keeping the stitches near the edge. (A coarse needle or pins will make holes that are impossible to remove.)

Working the appliqué

Work close zigzag stitch round the balloons, leaving a small gap at the bottom of each balloon. Push a little wadding into the balloons, using a knitting needle. Cut three 17cm (7in) lengths of 7mm (¼in)-wide ribbon. Tuck one end into each balloon and oversew. Make three small ribbon bows from the same ribbon and sew one under each balloon.

Applying trim

Making square corners Cut the broderie (eyelet) into four equal pieces. Lay two pieces together, right

sides facing (Fig 1). Fold one end at an angle of 45 degrees. Press. Stitch on the fold line. Trim off the corner. Open the broderie (eyelet) and press the seam open. Trim to make a neat square corner. Join all four pieces in the same way. Stitch the broderie (eyelet) 'frame' to the cushion piece.

Making mitred corners Apply 16mm (⅝in)-wide ribbon over the straight edges of the broderie (eyelet) square, mitring the corners neatly (Fig 2). Pin the ribbon in position, then edge-stitch along the inner edge. When you get to the corner, fold the ribbon back on itself and then diagonally to the side, making a right angle. Press the fold and then stitch on the crease through the ribbon and the fabric underneath. Open out the ribbon and press flat. Continue edge-stitching along the same inner edge until you reach the next corner. Work all four corners in the same way, then finish by sewing the outer edge of the ribbon all round.

Finishing

Bring the three ribbons from the balloons to one corner. Stitch down. Trim the ends so that the ribbons are of similar length, then cut each into a fish tail.

Make a bow from the remaining ribbon and sew over ribbons.

Make up the cushion as described in the box on page 24.

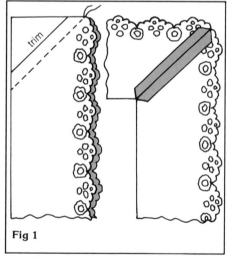

Fig 1

Fig 1 *Square corner*

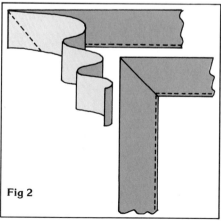

Fig 2

Fig 2 *Mitred corner*

Lilac heart

Materials required

Finished size 30×35cm (12×14in)

2 pieces of 40cm (16in) square white polyester satin fabric

1m (1⅛yd) of 10cm (4in)-wide white broderie anglaise (eyelet) edging

3m (3¼yd) of 7cm (2¾in)-wide white broderie anglaise (eyelet) edging

Light Orchid 430 single face polyester satin ribbons as follows: 1m (1⅛yd) of 23mm (⅞in)-wide and 13mm (½in)-wide; 35cm (14in) of 7mm (¼in)-wide

80cm (31in) of 23mm (⅞in)-wide Light Orchid 430 double face polyester satin ribbon

30×35cm (12×14in) heart-shaped cushion pad

Matching Drima sewing threads

Preparation

Use the cushion pad to draw a heart-shaped paper pattern. Cut out two shapes from white satin, adding 2cm (¾in) seam allowance all round. On one piece mark a vertical centre line in chalk.

Working the design

Cut two 28cm (11in) lengths of wide broderie (eyelet) edging. Lay the pieces together, fold one end diagonally and stitch to make a square corner (Fig 1). Sew to cushion piece with the decorative edge towards the bottom of the heart and aligning the join with the chalked centre line. Cut the remaining wide broderie (eyelet) into two equal lengths and stitch to make a square corner. Cut the narrowest Light Orchid 430 ribbon into two equal lengths and thread through the eyelet holes of both pieces of the broderie (eyelet), fastening ribbon ends off on the wrong side with two or three stitches. Position and stitch on the cushion so that the decorative edge is towards the top of the heart.

Cut both the 23mm and 13mm (⅞in and ½in)-wide ribbons in two pieces and cut and seam to make square corners. Appliqué the ribbons over the straight edges of the broderie (eyelet).

Finishing
Pleat the narrower broderie (eyelet) and baste to fit around the cushion. Apply the frill and make up the cushion as described in the box on page 24.

Make a bow from the double face Light Orchid 430 ribbon and hand-sew at top of heart.

Rose pink and cream cushion

Materials required
Finished size 24×30cm (9½×12in)
2 pieces of 28×33cm (11×13in) cream polyester satin fabric
4m (4½yd) of 4cm (1½in)-wide cream broderie anglaise (eyelet) edging
Pink 150 single face polyester satin ribbons as follows: 35cm (14in) of

39mm (1½in)-wide; 70cm (28in) of 23mm (⅞in)-wide and 16mm (⅝in)-wide
24×30cm (9½×12in) cushion pad
Matching Drima sewing threads

Preparation
Mark the centre line lengthwise along one piece of satin fabric. Cut six 35cm (14in) lengths of broderie (eyelet) edging.

Working the design
Baste a strip of broderie (eyelet) on both long sides of the cushion piece 2cm (¾in) from the edge. Lay a piece of the narrowest Pink 150 ribbon over both the straight edges and stitch along both edges of ribbon. Now lay a strip of broderie (eyelet) so that the decorative edge just overlaps the ribbons and baste.

Cut the 23mm (⅞in)-wide ribbon in two equal pieces and stitch over the straight edge of the broderie (eyelet) strips. Baste the last two strips of broderie (eyelet) so that they just overlap the ribbon. Appliqué the widest piece of ribbon down the centre, to cover the raw edges of the last two strips of broderie (eyelet).

Finishing
Cut the remaining broderie (eyelet) into four equal pieces. Make a square by following the technique described for Blue Balloons cushion (see also Fig 1). Pleat and baste the frill to fit around the cushion.

Apply the frill and make up the cushion as described in the box on page 24.

Cream and mint cushion

Materials required
Finished size 28.5cm (11¼in) square
2 pieces of 33cm (13in) square cream polyester satin fabric
1m (1⅛yd) of 57mm (2¼in)-wide and 60cm (24in) of 10mm (⅜in)-wide Mint 530 single face polyester satin ribbon
1m (1⅛yd) of 57mm (2¼in)-wide and 30cm (12in) of 10mm (⅜in)-wide Cream 815 single face polyester satin ribbon
1.20m (1⅜yd) of 5cm (2in)-wide cream broderie anglaise (eyelet) edging

Square cushion pad
Matching Drima sewing threads

Preparation
On one piece of satin fabric mark a line diagonally from corner to corner and then across again in the opposite direction, from corner to corner. Draw a plan on paper to size, following Fig 3. Cut out triangle A and segment B and use these as patterns for cutting ribbons.

Working the design
Work the four centre triangles first. From the wide ribbon cut two in Cream 815 and two in Mint 530, adding 6mm (¼in) turnings on the raw edges.

Position a Cream 815 triangle on the satin fabric, then turn raw edges under. Baste and stitch the bottom edge only. Prepare and position the second Cream 815 triangle to the right of the first, just overlapping the edge, and stitch the bottom edge and the left side. Now prepare and work the first Mint 530 triangle, again to the right, and stitch bottom edge and left side. Work the last Mint 530 triangle, machining all three sides.

Appliqué the 10mm (⅜in)-wide ribbon round the square, as shown in Fig 3, folding to make mitred corners (Fig 2). Cut and work the four segments B in the same way and in the same order as the triangles. Stitch top and bottom edges of piece 1, then top, bottom and left edge of piece 2, and so on.

Finishing
Make small bows with the remaining narrow Mint 530 ribbon and stitch on opposite corners, as shown in the picture.

Cut the broderie (eyelet) into four equal pieces. Make a square by following the technique described for Blue Balloons cushion (see also Fig 1). Stitch to cushion front, matching straight edge of trim to outer edge of ribbon appliqué.

Make up the cushion as described in the box on page 24.

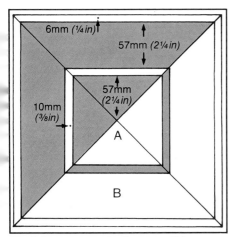

Fig 3 *Appliqué plan for Cream and Mint Cushion, showing triangles and segments*

6mm (¼in)
57mm (2¼in)
57mm (2¼in)
10mm (⅜in)
A
B

Medieval doublet

Glittering Jacquard ribbons and black velvet ribbons are appliquéd on to interfacing and lined with black satin to make this glamorous doublet.

The graph pattern (Fig 1) is for sizes 8-10 but as the doublet is loose fitting with no fastening, it will also fit up to size 14. The diagonal line on Front and Back pieces shows the direction of the appliquéd ribbons.

Estimating ribbon quantities

The ribbons used on the doublet are called trapunto Jacquards. When choosing ribbons for your own doublet, select three different widths, the narrowest about 23mm (⅞in) and the widest about 66mm (2⅝in). The black velvet ribbon used on the doublet is 23mm (⅞in) wide.

To estimate how much ribbon you require, first draw out the pattern pieces on squared paper, 1sq=5cm (2in). Mark the diagonal placement lines for ribbon, then the widths of the ribbons you intend using. Measure the total quantity required of each width.

Materials required

50×25cm (20×10in) black quilted or plain velvet fabric
75cm (30in) of 114cm (45in)-wide black satin fabric for lining
3.90m (4¼yd) of 8cm (3¼in)-wide fur trim or cut strips from fur fabric to this measurement
1m (1⅛yd) medium-weight iron-on interfacing
Ribbons as estimated
Squared pattern paper, 1sq=5cm (2in)

Preparation

Draw pattern pieces for Front, Back and Side on squared paper. The pattern does not include seam allowances. Lay the pattern pieces on the adhesive side of the interfacing and trace round, reversing them for Left and Right Fronts, Left and Right Backs, Left and Right Side Panels. This traced line is the stitching line.

Mark in the diagonal placement lines for ribbon. Draw a second line around each pattern shape on the interfacing 2cm (¾in) away. This is the cutting line.

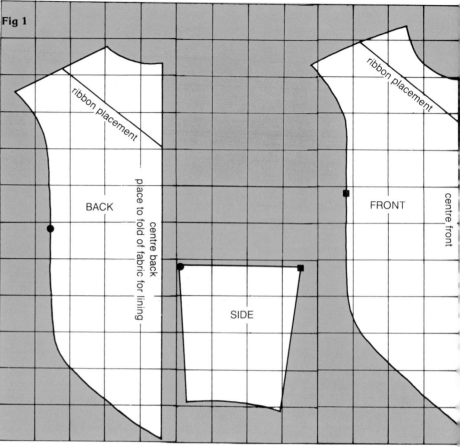

Fig 1 Graph pattern for Medieval Doublet, 1sq=5cm (2in). No seam allowance included

Working the side panels

From black velvet fabric, cut out two Side Panels, using the paper pattern and adding 2cm (¾in) seam allowance all round. Make sure the pile lies in the same direction on both pieces. Cut out and baste the interfacing sections to the wrong side of the velvet.

Working the appliqué

It is important for the two Fronts and the two Backs to be worked side by side so you can check that ribbons are in alignment. Check also that Fronts and Backs match up at the sides and on shoulder seams.

Lay the interfacing Fronts and Backs, adhesive side up, on a flat surface for working. Cut ribbon ends diagonally to fit the shape of the pattern pieces. Lay the first ribbon along the diagonal placement line and pin at both ends. Lay ribbons with edges touching, pinning them to the interfacing. When all ribbons are positioned, baste them to the interfacing. Turn the work over and press with a damp cloth and a hot

iron so that the ribbons adhere.

On the right side, machine-stitch along both edges of the ribbons. Work in the same direction each time as this helps to minimise warping of the ribbons. Remove basting stitches. Working on the wrong side, machine-stitch all round each piece of appliqué, working 1cm (⅜in) away from the stitching line.

Making up appliqué pieces

With right sides together, stitch Backs together on centre back seam. Join Backs to Fronts at shoulder seams.

Machine-stitch all round the two velvet Side Panel pieces, working 1cm (⅜in) from the stitching line. Trim away excess fabric 3mm (⅛in) from line of stitching. Stitch Side Panels to Fronts and Backs, matching small squares and dots (see Fig 1).

Making the lining

Pin the pattern pieces for Front and Side to doubled satin fabric and cut out two Fronts and two Sides, adding

2cm (¾in) seam allowance all round.
Pin Back pattern piece to doubled
fabric, with Centre Back along the
fold in the fabric. Cut out Back in
one piece so that there is no Centre
Back seam, but add 2cm (¾in) seam
allowance on all other edges.

With right sides together, stitch
Fronts to Back at shoulder seams.
Stitch Front and Back side seams to
Side Panels. Press seams open.

Pin the lining, right side to right
side of fabric, into the doublet. Baste,
then stitch round on Front, Back and
armhole edges, leaving the seam
open on the Back hem for turning.
Turn garment to right side. Lightly
press the seam all round. Close open
seam with hand-sewing.

Finishing

Baste right side of fur trim to right
side of garment along all edges and
armholes. Stitch, then fold and baste
trim to inside of garment so that an
equal amount of fur shows on the
right and wrong side. Join ends.
Hand-sew trim to inside of garment.

Designed by Jackie Burchall

Pink and green table set

Applying bands of ribbons in toning colours is one of the prettiest ways of decorating home linens – not only tablecloths, table-mats and napkins but also curtains, bedspreads and hand towels. It is important that washable, non-iron, colourfast polyester ribbons are used for items which will be laundered frequently.

The table set pictured is for a circular table and to achieve the ribbon-banded decoration, the tablecloth has been designed as an octagon (eight-sided shape). This has enabled the ribbons to be applied smooth and flat, which would be impossible on a circular cloth. The matching napkins, table-mats and roll holder are also octagon-shaped.

Tablecloth and napkins

Materials required

For a cloth 152cm (60in) diameter and six napkins 42cm (16½in) diameter

157cm *(62in)* square pale green polyester/cotton fabric

6 pieces of 46cm *(18in)* square pale pink polyester/cotton fabric

Single face polyester satin ribbons as follows:

For the tablecloth edging: 5.20m *(5¾yd)* of 39mm *(1½in)*-wide Pink 150; 4.80m *(5¼yd)* of 10mm *(⅜in)*-wide Pink 150; 4.80m *(5¼yd)* of 10mm *(⅜in)*-wide Ice Mint 510; 4.60m *(5yd)* of 7mm *(¼in)*-wide Light Pink 117

For the tablecloth centre: 1m *(1⅛yd)* of 7mm *(¼in)*-wide Pink 150 and Ice Mint 510

For the napkins: 8.10m *(8⅞yd)* of 23mm *(⅞in)*-wide Mint 530; 6.85m *(7½yd)* of 10mm *(⅜in)*-wide Mint 530

Matching Drima sewing threads

Preparation

Measure the vertical centre and the horizontal centre of the green fabric, then mark with lines of basting or chalk pencil (Fig 1). Mark the diagonals. Measure and mark points on the diagonal lines 78cm *(31in)* from the centre. With chalk pencil lines join the vertical and horizontal lines with these points. Draw the inner octagon in the same way, measuring and marking points on the diagonal lines 16.5cm *(6½in)* from the centre. Cut out the octagonal cloth.

The six napkins are worked in the same way, but without the central appliquéd octagon.

Working the design

The techniques are the same for cloth, napkins and roll holder.

Press a narrow hem all round the octagon to the right side. Baste the wide Pink 150 ribbon over the cloth's hem, on the right side, folding corners to follow the angle. Machine-stitch on both edges, working in the same direction both times and taking care not to stretch the fabric or the ribbon. Remove basting threads before pressing with a cool iron but using lots of pressure.

Press a narrow hem all round on the napkins. Then complete the appliqué bands as follows.

On the cloth, from the hem inwards: 39mm *(1½in)*-wide Pink 150 as described above, then a space of 6mm *(¼in)*. Next, the 10mm *(⅜in)*-wide Pink 150, with Ice Mint 510 laid edge to edge against the Pink 150. Leave a gap of 6mm *(¼in)*, then apply the 7mm *(¼in)*-wide Light Pink 117 ribbon.

For the tablecloth centre, baste and stitch the 7mm *(¼in)*-wide Pink 150 ribbon on the octagon marked. Stitch the Ice Mint 510 ribbon on the inside edge of the Pink ribbon.

On the napkins, appliqué the 23mm *(⅞in)*-wide Mint 530 on the hem, then set the 10mm *(⅜in)*-wide Mint 530 6mm *(¼in)* away.

Offray Design Studio

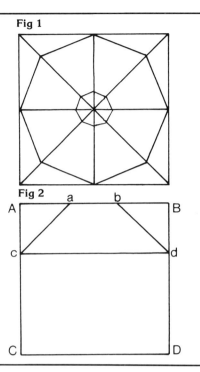

Fig 1

Fig 2

Fig 1 *Making octagons on a square*

Fig 2 *For the coffeepot cosy and egg cosy shape, measure A-B and mark into thirds, (a) and (b). Mark A-a measurement on line A-C, (c). Mark b-B measurement on line B-D, (d). Join lines*

Table-mats

Materials required
For each table-mat, finished size 25cm (10in) diameter
26cm *(10½in)* square white quilted cotton fabric
26cm *(10½in)* square pale pink or green polyester/cotton fabric
1.40m *(1½yd)* of 7mm *(¼in)*-wide Pink 150, Mint 530, Ice Mint 510 double face polyester satin ribbons

Preparation
Cut quilting and backing fabric into octagons (Fig 1).

Working the design
Stitch together the quilting and backing fabric, right sides facing, on seven sides, taking 6mm *(¼in)* seams. Turn to right side and close eighth side with hand-sewing. Make ribbons into a folded plait (see page 23, Fig 2) and hand-sew round mat.

Roll holder

Materials required
Finished size 37cm (14½in) diameter
2 pieces of 39cm *(15½in)* square pale pink polyester/cotton fabric
2.30m *(2½yd)* of 10mm *(⅜in)*-wide Mint 530 single face polyester satin ribbon
2m *(2¼yd)* of 7mm *(¼in)* wide Mint 530 double face polyester satin ribbon

Preparation
Cut both squares of fabric into octagons as for tablecloth and napkins (see also Fig 1).

Working the design
Press a narrow hem to the right side on both pieces of fabric. Stitch the 10mm *(⅜in)*-wide Mint 530 ribbon over the hem, on the right side.

Lay one octagon on the other, ribbon uppermost, and pin together. Mark into eight segments with chalk pencil lines, then baste along the lines. Machine-stitch the two octagons together on the segment lines. Cut the narrower Mint 530 ribbon into eight pieces. Stitch half-way along each segment on the appliquéd hem for ties.

Cosies

Materials required
For coffeepot cosy, finished size 29 × 31cm (11½ × 12½in)
2 pieces of 31×33cm *(12½ × 13½in)* white quilted cotton fabric
2 pieces of 31×33cm *(12½ × 13½in)* pale pink or green polyester/cotton lining fabric
For appliqué: 1.40m *(1½yd)* of 7mm *(¼in)*-wide Mint 530 and Pink 150 single face polyester satin ribbons
For plait trim: 1m *(1⅛yd)* of 7mm *(¼in)*-wide Pink 150, Mint 530 and Ice Mint 510 double face polyester satin ribbons
For six egg cosies, finished size 10cm (4in) square
12 pieces of 11cm *(4½in)* square white quilted cotton fabric
12 pieces of 11cm *(4½in)* square pale pink or green polyester/cotton lining fabric
1.20m *(1⅜yd)* of 7mm *(¼in)*-wide Pink 150 and Mint 530 single face polyester satin ribbons

Preparation
For both large and small cosies, lay squares of quilting and fabric together in pairs and trim off the corners (Fig 2).

Working the design
Apply ribbon trims to the quilted pieces. On the coffeepot cosy, stitch Pink 150 ribbon 5cm *(2in)* from the bottom edge, with Mint 530 15mm *(⅝in)* away. Leave a space of 6cm *(2½in)*, then apply the Mint 530 ribbon, with the Pink 150 15mm *(⅝in)* away. On the egg cosies, appliqué the Pink 150 ribbon 23mm *(⅞in)* from the bottom edge, with the Mint 530 15mm *(⅝in)* away.

Place two quilted cosy pieces together, right sides facing, and stitch sides and top. Trim seams and turn to right side. Make up linings in the same way. Insert linings, turn the bottom edge hems inside and machine-stitch. Trim the bottom edge of the coffeepot cosy with a ribbon folded plait (see page 23, Fig 2).

Night specials

By applying narrow ribbons to wider ribbons, interesting contrasts can be achieved. This technique has been used on the evening bag and belt pictured. The belt is shaped to cinch the waist and is back-fastening.

Appliquéd belt

Materials required

For a 71cm (28in) waist

1m×28cm *(1⅛yd×11in)* black satin fabric

30cm *(12in)* square of same fabric for bias binding

50×28cm *(20×11in)* pelmet-weight interfacing

Single face polyester satin ribbons for appliqué and rosette as follows: 3.60m *(4yd)* of 13mm *(½in)*-wide White 029; 1.50m *(1⅝yd)* of 3mm *(⅛in)*-wide Black 030; 2m *(2¼yd)* of 13mm *(½in)*-wide Black 030; 4.80m *(5¼yd)* of 3mm *(⅛in)*-wide Red 250

3 pairs of hooks and eyes

Matching Drima sewing threads

Squared pattern paper, 1sq=2.5cm *(1in)*

Preparation

Copy the graph pattern for the belt Front and Back pieces (Fig 1) on to the squared paper to make your pattern. To adapt the pattern to a larger or smaller waist measurement, cut on the lines X-X and spread or overlap the pieces as required. You have sufficient Red, White and 13mm *(½in)*-wide Black ribbons for two sizes larger − waists 73.5cm *(29in)* and 76cm *(30in)* − but you will need more of the 3mm *(⅛in)*-wide Black: allow an extra 50cm *(20in)*.

Cut the belt Front and Back pieces four times from satin fabric and twice from interfacing, adding 12mm *(½in)* seam allowance on the curved waist seams (marked on the pattern with a broken line). Mark the ribbon placement lines (1,2,3) on the fabric in basting thread. Baste a satin piece, right side up, to each of the corresponding interfacing pieces.

Cut the square of satin fabric into bias strips 2.5cm *(1in)* wide and join for bias binding.

Working the appliqué

Work on the belt Front pieces first. Cut three pieces of White ribbon for each Front piece, measuring from the curved waist seam to Centre Front. Baste and stitch ribbons 1 and 2 (see Fig 1) on both pieces. Using white thread and zigzag stitch sew narrow Black ribbon down the centre of ribbons 1 and 2. Now baste and stitch White ribbon 3 over the point where 1 and 2 touch and as shown on the pattern (Fig 1). Stitch narrow Black ribbon down the centre as before, using white thread and zigzag stitch. Work the appliqué on the Back belt pieces to match.

Stitch the two Fronts to the two Backs along the curved waist seams. Clip into the seam allowance and trim back to 6mm *(¼in)*.

Cut 2.70m *(3yd)* of Red ribbon into three equal pieces. Work into a flat plait (see page 23, Fig 1). Hand-sew the plait on both edges of the central White ribbon on both belt pieces, working from Centre Front to Centre Back.

Lining the belt

Stitch the remaining satin fabric pieces together on the curved waist seams. Baste the lining to the wrong side of the belt pieces. Bind all the edges of both pieces with bias satin strips, working first on the right side and then taking the bias over to the wrong side. Catch the bias to the lining with neat hand-sewing.

Finishing

Oversew the belt Fronts together. Stitch hooks and eyes on the belt Backs.

With the remaining ribbons make a rosette for the front of the belt, sewing the ribbons into loops and leaving long streamer ends. Cut the ends diagonally to prevent fraying. You will have sufficient ribbons to make a small matching rosette for the front of the evening bag (see instructions for finishing the bag).

Evening bag

Materials required

Finished size 17×33cm (6¾×13in)

59×35cm *(23¼×14in)* black satin fabric

Same quantity of polyester wadding, lining and iron-on interfacing

20cm *(8in)* square of the same black satin fabric for covering piping cord

1m *(1⅛yd)* piping cord

Single face polyester satin ribbons as follows: 1.50m *(1⅝yd)* of 13mm *(½in)*-wide White 029; 53cm *(21in)* of 3mm *(⅛in)*-wide Black 030; 1.50m *(1⅝yd)* of 3mm *(⅛in)*-wide Red 250

For optional carrying strap, allow 4m *(4½yd)* of 3mm *(⅛in)*-wide Black 030

Large press fastener

Matching Drima sewing threads

Squared pattern paper, 1sq=2.5cm *(1in)*

Preparation

Copy the graph pattern for the bag (Fig 1) on to the squared paper. Mark in the Fold Lines. Use the pattern to cut out the bag shape in black satin fabric, in lining, in iron-on interfacing and in wadding, adding 12mm *(½in)* seam allowance all round. Mark the centre of the flap with a row of basting stitches. Iron the interfacing on to the back of the satin piece, then baste on the wadding. Cut the square of black satin into bias strips 2.5cm *(1in)* wide, join them and cover the piping cord.

Working the appliqué

Baste a piece of White ribbon on the centre line of basting on the bag flap from the Flap Fold Line to the edge of the seam allowance on the curved flap edge. This is ribbon 1. Baste a piece of White ribbon each side of ribbon 1, 2cm *(¾in)* away. These are ribbons 2 and 3. Stitch all three ribbons on both edges. Now apply a piece of Black ribbon down the centre of ribbon 1, using white thread and zigzag stitch.

Baste White ribbons 4 and 5 5cm

Designed by Jennifer Banhar

(2in) away from ribbons 2 and 3. Stitch both on both edges. Baste White ribbons 6 and 7 2cm (¾in) away from ribbons 4 and 5 and stitch. Using white thread, zigzag stitch Black ribbon down the centre of ribbons 4 and 5. Remove all basting threads.

Cut the Red ribbon into three equal pieces. Work into a flat plait (see page 23, Fig 1). Cut the plait in two and secure the ends with a few stitches. Hand-sew the plaits down the outside edge of ribbons 2 and 3. To finish the appliqué, machine-stitch White ribbon along the flap fold to cover the raw ends of the applied ribbons.

Making up the bag

Pin and baste the prepared piping on the right side of fabric across the edge of the pocket, raw edges together. Machine-stitch from the right side. Pin and baste piping round the curved flap in the same way and stitch. Fold the bag on the Pocket Fold Line, right sides together. Baste and stitch the side seams.

Remove basting threads. Trim back the wadding seam allowance to 6mm (¼in). Turn bag to right side. If you are making the carrying strap, flat-plait the remaining Black ribbon and stitch the plait inside the pocket on both sides.

Finishing

Baste and stitch the side seams of the lining piece, right sides together, and insert the lining into the bag. Slip-stitch the lining in place. Sew on the press fastener to close.

Make a ribbon rosette from 15cm (6in) pieces of 13mm (½in)-wide Black 030 and White 029 ribbons together with a piece of 3mm (⅛in)-wide Red 250 ribbon. Stitch the rosette to the bag flap.

Fig 1 *Graph pattern for Belt and Bag, 1sq = 2.5cm (1in)*

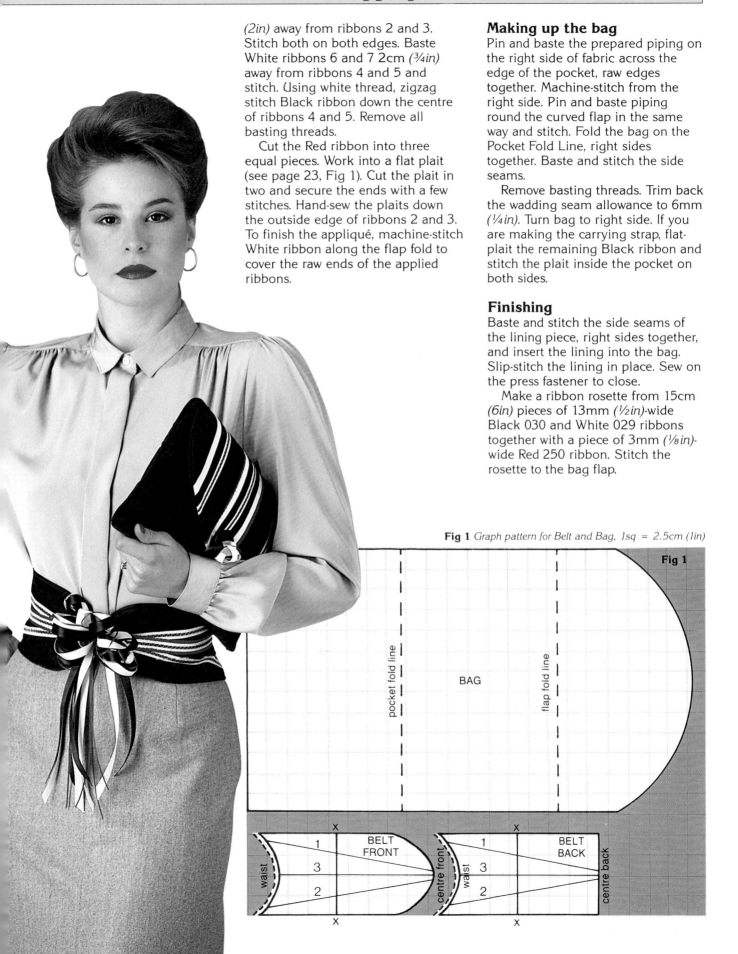

Lace and ribbon quilt

Lace and ribbons are lovely materials to work with in appliqué. As you are working with two selvedges, stitching is easy and the work grows quickly. The panel of appliqué in the picture is for a quilt made up of 23cm (9in) squares of lace and ribbons. The centre square shown is appliquéd with antique cotton lace set around a square of ribbon weaving.

The quilt is made up of 45 whole squares and 22 half squares (see Fig 1). You could vary all the appliqué squares, mixing and matching together laces and ribbons of different widths and colour tones.

Materials required

Finished size 255×152cm (100×60in)
2.60m (2⅞yd) of 157cm (62in)-wide cream polyester cotton or satin for backing
4.60m (5yd) of 114cm (45in)-wide thin cream cotton fabric for mounting appliqué
2.60m (2⅞yd) of 157cm (62in)-wide polyester wadding (optional)
Assorted laces and ribbons of different widths in cream, tan and ivory colour ranges*
14m (15⅜yd) of 16mm (⅝in)-wide Cream 815 single face polyester satin ribbon for joining squares
Lace trim (optional – see Edging the quilt)
Matching Drima sewing threads
*Each square of appliqué takes nine pieces of 2.5cm (1in)-wide lace or ribbon, so allow a total of 2.30m (2½yd) per square

Preparation

Cut the thin cotton into 56 squares. Cut 11 of the squares in half on the diagonal. Work each square or half square separately. Cut ribbons and lace into 23cm (9in) lengths.

Working the design

Pin and baste ribbons and lace to the squares, edges touching. You can mix lace and ribbons of different widths and colours. If you have odd scraps of lace net, try basting a piece over the backing square without ribbons or lace strips for a textural contrast. Work all the squares and half squares. Trim the backing fabric to the edges of the appliqué.

Joining squares

Lay two squares together, right sides facing. Join along one edge with large oversewing stitches, worked right on the edge, as a basting. Join enough squares to make a strip, then press on the right side. Stitch over the basted seam with zigzag stitches.

Join all the squares together, with the half squares on the edges of the quilt. Stitch the 16mm (⅝in)-wide Cream 815 ribbon over the joins with straight stitches along both edges of the ribbons.

Finishing

Lay the backing fabric wrong side up. If you are using polyester wadding, place this on the backing. Lay the appliqué on top, right side up. Pin the corners, then the edges. Thread the needle with a doubled length of thread. Tie a knot on the end. Make two or three stitches right through the appliqué top to the backing, at the corners of all the squares. Trim the knot and finish on the wrong side with a back stitch to secure. These are called 'quilting ties'.

If you prefer a decorative tie, use 1.5mm (1/16 in)-wide Cream 815 ribbon. Work from the right side and bring the needle back to the right side, tying the ends in a tight bow.

Edging the quilt

The quilt may be edged in a variety of ways. A double frill of cream lace would look very glamorous. You would need about 16.50m (18yd) to make a double layer of pre-frilled lace edging. Alternatively, a single frill of cream broderie anglaise (eyelet) might be used; for this you would need 8.25m (9yd). A simple lace insert with a ribbon to match the quilt could be applied to the edge; again, allow 8.25m (9yd) of each. Or perhaps a single wide band of Cream 815 satin ribbon with mitred corners might be used; you would need 8.25m (9yd) of 39mm (1½in)-wide ribbon.

Having applied the trim of your choice, turn the edges of the backing fabric under and hand-hem to the back of the quilt.

Designed by Audrey Vincente Dean

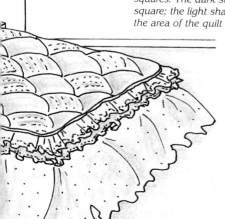

Fig 1 *Diagram of the Lace and Ribbon Quilt, made up of 45 whole squares and 22 half squares. The dark shaded area is the centre square; the light shaded rectangle represents the area of the quilt shown in the picture*

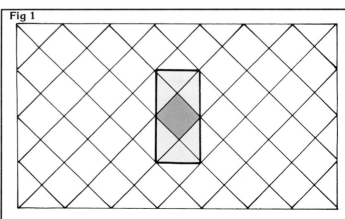

Fig 1

Appliqué clown

This colourful clown picture uses two ribboncraft techniques — appliqué and ribbon weaving. A variety of different ribbons has been used — striped grosgrains, some with Lurex, plain and spotted grosgrain ribbons and gold Lurex ribbon. If you cannot exactly match the ribbons used, choose clear primary colours and one or two pastel colours to achieve the same bright effect. The finished picture is 50cm *(20in)* square. The pattern is shown overleaf.

Materials required

50cm *(20in)* square three-ply wood for backing board
70cm *(28in)* square dark blue polyester/cotton fabric
20×30cm *(8×12in)* white polyester/cotton fabric
50×62cm *(20×24½in)* lightweight iron-on interfacing
Ribbons — see key to pattern overleaf for type and quantity
Anchor stranded embroidery threads in red, bright green, dark blue
Drima sewing threads to match ribbons and fabrics
Basting thread, strong button thread
Latex fabric adhesive, thumbtacks
Squared pattern paper, 1sq=4cm *(1½in)*
Tracing paper, dressmakers' carbon paper

Preparing the pattern

Draw the pattern (Fig 1 overleaf) up to full size on the squared pattern paper. To do this, first join the blue marks on the edge of the pattern both horizontally and vertically so that you have a squared grid over the pattern. Now copy the picture of the clown on to your squared paper, marking in all the symbols.

You will see that the left side of the clown pattern shows the first stage of laying ribbons and the right side shows the second stage, when ribbons are interwoven. The finished picture has left and right sides exactly the same.

The clown's face is given life-size (Fig 2 overleaf) and this should be traced. The hands and feet should be traced from your full-size pattern.

Pin and weave brightly coloured ribbons — and watch the clown picture grow

Preparing the fabric

Iron all creases from fabrics. Measure and mark the centre of the blue fabric with threads. Measure from the centre a 50cm *(20in)* square. Mark the square with threads. Cut a 50cm *(20in)* square of iron-on interfacing. Iron it on to the wrong side of the blue fabric, matching edges to the thread lines. Work zigzag stitch round the outside edge of the fabric to prevent fraying. Mount the white fabric in the same way.

From white fabric, cut clown's face and from doubled fabric cut the hands and feet (two of each). Pin the blue fabric to the backing board with thumbtacks. Using the dressmakers' carbon paper, trace all the lines of the clown pattern on to the fabric, or use the tissue paper and thread method (see page 8).

Working the design

You will see that the ribbons are interwoven on the clown's trousers but are worked as plain appliqué on the body and arms.

Measure each ribbon carefully. Where ribbons go right to the edge of the picture, add 1cm *(⅜in)* to the length. Cut ribbons to follow curves exactly and add 2cm *(¾in)* to the length of each. Apply the legs and body ribbons first, working left and right sides together and taking them under the neck frill because the neck frill ribbons are not to be stitched down. Work the arm ribbons next.

Pin each ribbon down at both ends, edges touching. Note that the ribbons for the hair and neck frill overlap slightly to follow the curve of the clown's head.

When stage 1 ribbons are pinned on the body, arms and legs, work stage 2, weaving ribbons in and out of the stage 1 ribbons. Again pin both ends. When all ribbons are placed, baste them to the blue background fabric, keeping stitches close to the edges of the ribbons so that your needle does not mark the ribbons. Remove the pins and thumbtacks.

Using matching threads, machine-

Key to pattern

Pattern symbols	Ribbon	Width	Quantity
■	blue grosgrain	16mm (⅝in)	1.60m (1¾yd)
▲	red/navy stripe grosgrain	23mm (⅞in)	70cm (28in)
✚	red grosgrain	16mm (⅝in)	1.60m (1¾yd)
★	white spots/red grosgrain	16mm (⅝in)	60cm (24in)
▢	white spots/blue grosgrain	16mm (⅝in)	60cm (24in)
✸	silver Lurex/pink stripe	10mm (⅜in)	1.70m (1⅞yd)
∧	gold Lurex/pink edge	10mm (⅜in)	1.40m (1½yd)
✳	rainbow stripe/Lurex	23mm (⅞in)	3.50m (3⅞yd)
◠	pastel stripe/Lurex	23mm (⅞in)	1.40m (1½yd)
❘	red/white stripe	39mm (1½in)	55cm (22in)

stitch ribbon edges. Do not stitch down the ribbon woven areas. Stitch only the ribbons laid from the edge of the weaving to the edge of the picture.

On the neck frill, note that only the ribbon ends that go under the clown's head are stitched down. The other ends and the sides are left free.

Finishing

Embroider the features on the clown's face in Stem stitch, using four strands of thread together. Work the eyebrows, the outlines of the eye, and the nose in dark blue; work the pupils in green and the mouth in red. Using machine zigzag stitch, apply the face, hands and feet to the clown picture. Work close zigzag stitch all round the clown's body.

Apply the ribbon for the border, mitring the corners (see page 26, Fig 2, for technique). Stitch the ribbons on both edges. Pull all loose thread ends through to the wrong side to neaten off. Press if necessary.

Lay the backing board on the wrong side of the picture and lace the picture to the board with strong button thread. Work lacing horizontally and vertically, keeping the picture square and as smooth as possible. The picture can be framed for hanging or hung just as it is without a frame.

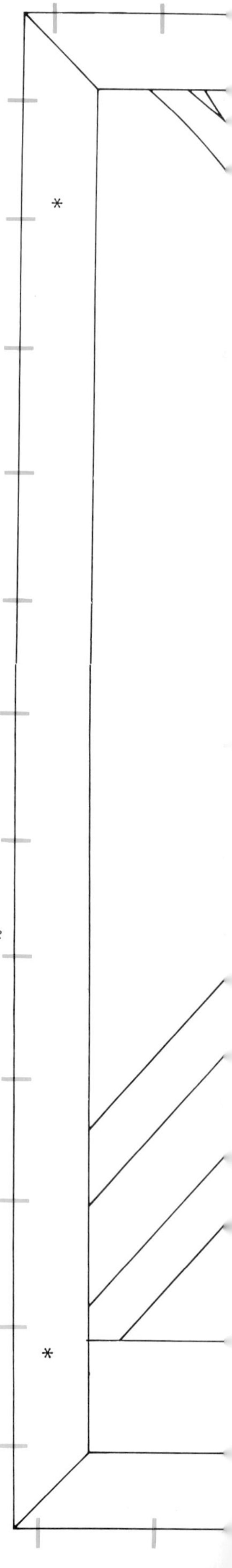

Fig 1 *The clown pattern is to a scale of 1sq = 4cm (1½in). The left side shows the first stage of laying the ribbons; the right side shows the ribbons interwoven in the second stage*

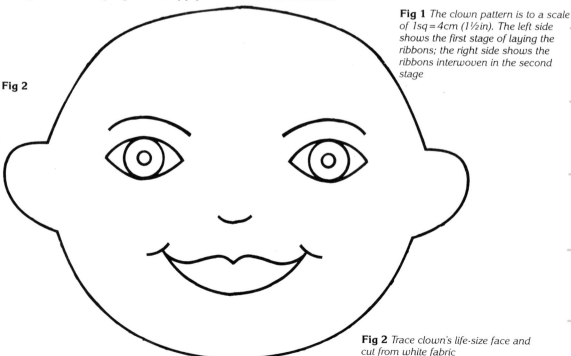

Fig 2 *Trace clown's life-size face and cut from white fabric*

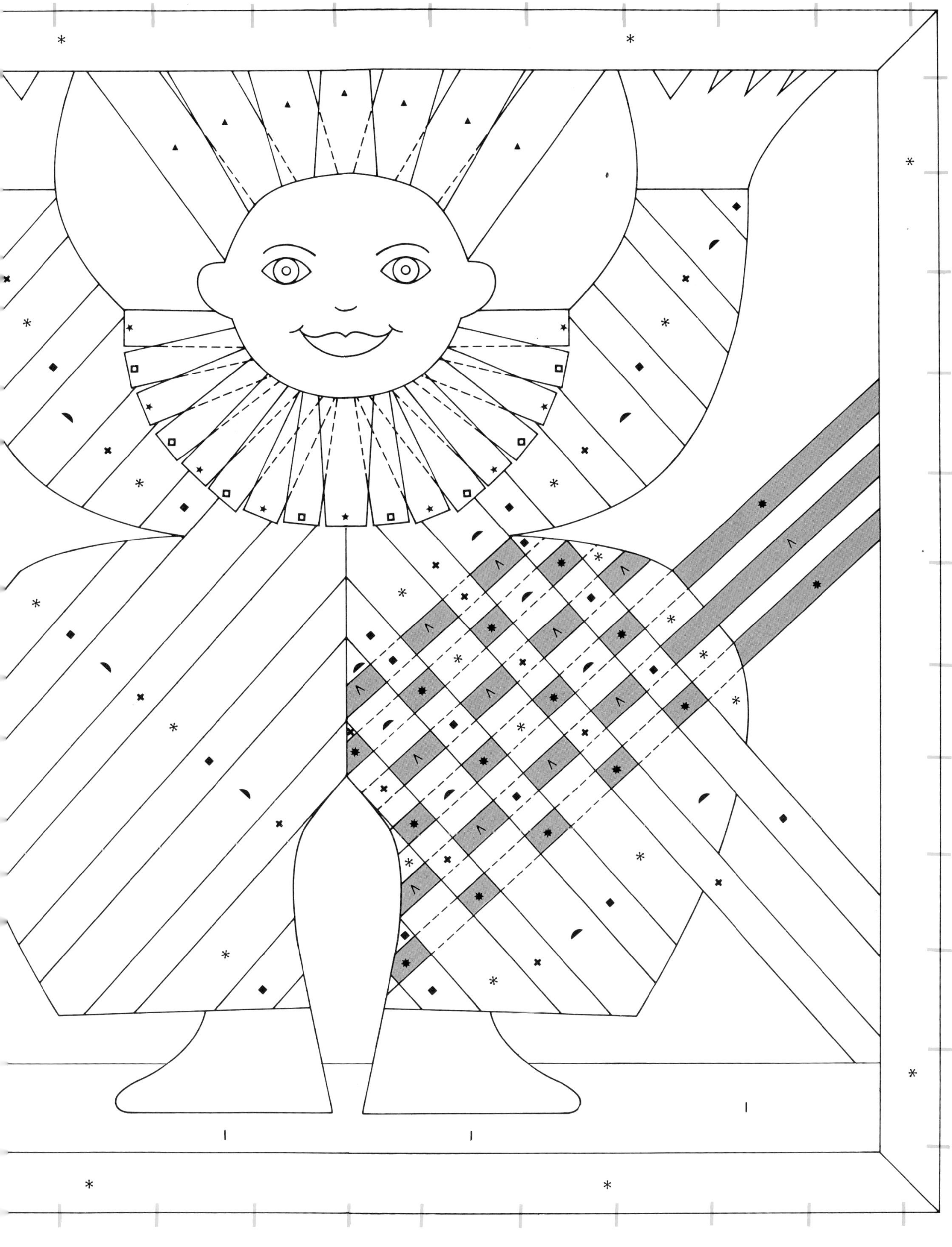

Ribbon Quilting

Ribbon quilting can have two applications. On the beautiful rose-trimmed bedcover illustrated, ribbons have been machine-quilted in a diamond pattern on quilted broderie anglaise (eyelet) fabric to give a luxurious, raised effect. Ribbon quilting can also mean ribbon 'piecing', where ribbons are used to make up patchwork blocks, such as the popular Log Cabin pattern. A child's comforter quilt made of ribbon, fabric and broderie (eyelet) in the Log Cabin pattern is shown overleaf.

Ribbons make beautiful rooms maginative use of polyester ribbons n home decor is effectively llustrated here. The techniques required to make similar accessories and furnishings are to be found in this book.

Pictures and mirrors Glue touch-and-fasten spots to the back of frames and to wide ribbons for a pretty hanging method. Finish with a bunch of ribbons tied in a bow. On the table, two picture frames are trimmed with ribbon-threaded broderie anglaise (eyelet) edging. The rectangular frame has dressmaker roses (see pages 6-7) at two corners; the heart-shaped frame

is finished with a small ribbon bow. Another frame is covered in ribbon weaving (see pages 46-49 and page 53 for how to make frames).

Tables Make square or round cloths for small tables and trim with ribbon-threaded broderie anglaise (eyelet) edging.

Conversation pieces Small boxes covered with fabric can be trimmed with dressmaker roses for colour-co-ordinated accessories. Make a plaited bookmark from matching ribbons. The basket on the table illustrated is filled with fresh gypsophila flowers and ribbon roses (see pages 54-55) and decorated with dressmaker roses and ribbon bows.

Cushions The three cushions illustrated are colour-co-ordinated with ribbons to match the overall scheme. The bolster pillow and the frilled square cushion are appliquéd with ribbon bands on quilted broderie anglaise (eyelet) fabric and trimmed with clusters of dressmaker roses. The blue cushion is ribbon woven.

Bedcover Machine-quilted broderie anglaise (eyelet) fabric is diamond-quilted with 23mm (⅞in)-wide satin ribbons and finished at the points of the diamonds with bows and dressmaker roses. Five appliqué bands of ribbons and a wide broderie anglaise (eyelet) frill finish the edges.

Quick-make lampshade cover

The pretty lampshade cover illustrated is made of white broderie anglaise (eyelet) fabric and trimmed with pink dressmaker roses.

Materials required
White lampshade
Broderie anglaise (eyelet) fabric (estimate quantity as below)
4cm (1½in)-wide broderie anglaise (eyelet) insert edging and 10mm (⅜in)-wide Pink 150 single face polyester satin ribbon (estimate quantities as below)
For roses and loops: 2m (2¼yd) of 23mm (⅞in)-wide single face and 1.50m (1⅝yd) of 3mm (⅛in)-wide double face Pink 150 polyester satin ribbon
Matching Drima sewing threads

Estimating fabric and ribbon quantities
To determine the amount of fabric required for the lampshade cover, measure round the base of the shade and double the measurement. Measure from the top of the shade to the base and add 2.5cm (1in). Buy broderie anglaise (eyelet) fabric to these measurements. To estimate the broderie anglaise (eyelet) insert edging required, measure round the top of the

shade and add 2.5cm (1in). You will need this same quantity of 10mm (⅜in)-wide Pink 150 ribbon.

Making the cover
Join the short ends of the broderie (eyelet) fabric. Neaten the seam allowance edges. Press a 6mm (¼in) fold to the right side along the top edge. Gather the top edge of the cover to fit the circumference of the lampshade's top edge.

Thread the 10mm (⅜in)-wide ribbon through the broderie (eyelet) insert edging. Stitch to the top of the cover, along both edges and over the gathering stitches. Turn the ends under and hand-sew. Sew the ribbon ends together.

Make 12 dressmaker roses (see pages 6-7). Sew in groups of three round the top of the cover, placing one group over the join in the broderie (eyelet) insert edging. Cut the narrow ribbon into four pieces. Sew small loops of ribbon among the roses and leave 15cm (6in) streamers.

Offray Design Studio

Log Cabin comforter quilt

Log Cabin is one of the traditional American quilting patterns and is said to have been inspired by the play of firelight on the dark cabin walls.

The quilt pictured is made using the Log Cabin technique, but ribbons provide additional pattern interest.

Materials required

Finished size 97 × 73cm (38 × 29in)
1m *(1⅛yd)* of 120cm *(48in)*-wide washable lining fabric
1.40m *(1½yd)* of 120cm *(48in)*-wide fine white cotton
75cm *(30in)* of 1m *(1⅛yd)*-wide polyester wadding

Patchwork materials:

20cm *(8in)* of 114cm *(45in)*-wide white self-spotted fabric
8m *(8¾yd)* of 23mm *(⅞in)*-wide pink/white gingham check taffeta ribbon
9.50m *(10½yd)* of 23mm *(⅞in)*-wide pink taffeta ribbon
12m *(13¼yd)* of 23mm *(⅞in)*-wide white taffeta ribbon
12m *(13¼yd)* of 13mm *(½in)*-wide woven polyester ribbon with hearts motif
9.50m *(10½yd)* of 3cm *(1⅛in)*-wide white broderie anglaise (eyelet) edging
1.85m *(2yd)* of 39mm *(1½in)*-wide Pink 150 polyester satin ribbon
1.85m *(2yd)* of 39mm *(1½in)*-wide white or pink lace net

For finishing quilt:

4m *(4½yd)* of 2.5cm *(1in)*-wide broderie anglaise (eyelet) insert edging
4.30m *(4¾yd)* of 10mm *(⅜in)*-wide Pink 150 polyester satin ribbon
1 skein Anchor stranded embroidery thread in white

Preparation

The quilt is made up of 48 blocks, each 12cm *(4¾in)* square.

Cut 48 15cm *(6in)* squares of fine white cotton, for patchwork bases, and measure and mark the centre of each.

Cut 48 39mm *(1½in)* squares of the wide Pink 150 ribbon and cut squares of lace net to cover. Pin them together in the centre of the cotton squares. Cut the white spotted fabric into strips the same width as the pink gingham ribbon.

Note: in this project, ribbons are folded on the long edge for sewing in the same way as raw edges of fabric.

Working the design

The ribbons and fabric strips are hand-sewn or machine-stitched round the central pink square, right sides facing, then pressed back.

Round 1 Strip 1: cut a 5cm *(2in)* length of white spotted fabric. Stitch right sides to right sides along bottom edge of pink square, taking a 3mm *(⅛in)* seam. Press back flat. Strip 2: cut a second strip of spotted fabric 5.5cm *(2⅛in)* long and position down the left side of the square. The top edge of the strip should extend 3mm *(⅛in)* beyond the top edge of the ribbon square. Stitch right sides to right sides, as before. Press. Strip 3: cut pink gingham ribbon to go along the top of the pink square, measuring and cutting so that the ribbon extends 3mm *(⅛in)* beyond the pink square on the right and 3mm *(⅛in)* beyond the unstitched edge of Strip 2. Complete the first round by cutting and stitching Strip 4, which is a second strip of pink gingham ribbon. As you can now see, each strip overlaps the previous strip and is overlapped by the subsequent strip.
Round 2 Following the same technique of measuring and sewing strips, work in these fabrics and ribbons: Strips 1 and 2: broderie anglaise (eyelet). Fold under decorative edge to achieve the same width as the gingham ribbon. Strips 3 and 4: pink taffeta ribbon.
Round 3 Strips 1 and 2: white taffeta

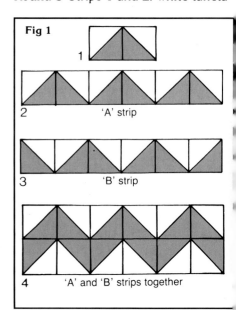

Fig 1 *Joining blocks*

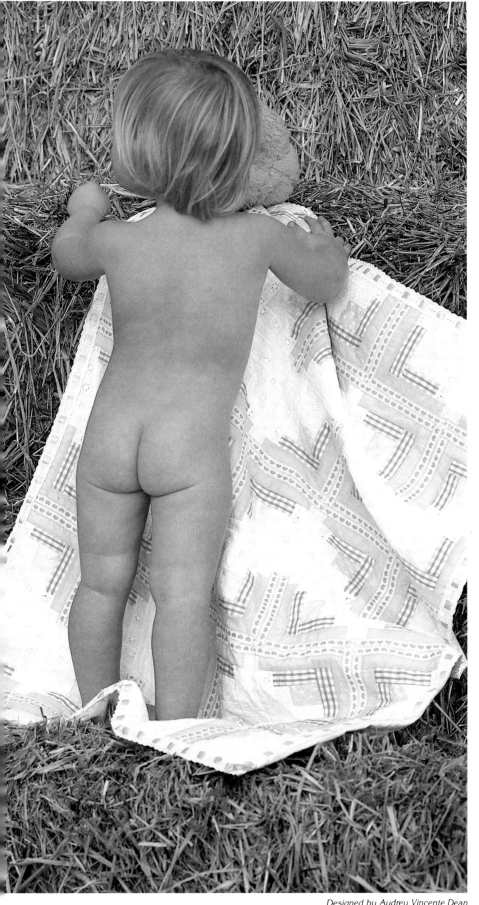

ribbon folded to the same width as the hearts ribbon. Strips 3 and 4: hearts ribbon, set 15mm (⅝in) away from the stitched edge of the pink taffeta ribbon in round 2. Stitch hearts ribbon with zigzag stitch.

Make up 48 blocks in the same way. Press blocks. Trim backing fabric to the edges of the block.

Joining blocks

Pairs of blocks are joined with zigzag machine-stitch working on the right side. As you can see from the pictures, blocks are joined so that a chevron pattern is achieved in the finished quilt. To work this, proceed as follows (and see Fig 1):
1. Join 40 blocks in pairs, 'dark' side to 'dark' side (ie, the dark pink side).
2. Join three of these pairs together on the 'light' sides (ie, the white sides) to form a strip of six blocks. Make four strips of six blocks in this way. These will be referred to as 'A' strips.
3. Join two pairs of blocks on the light sides, then add a single block at each end, again joining on the light sides. Make four strips in this way. These will be referred to as 'B' strips.
4. Lay an 'A' strip with a 'B' strip, dark sides of strips together. Pin the seam, right sides facing, then oversew, for basting, together.
5. Press the seam open and zigzag stitch the edges together on the right side. Remove basting oversewing stitches.

Make up the quilt in strips of 'A' and 'B' in this way.

Finishing

Stitch broderic (cyelet) insert edgling round the edges of the quilt, mitring corners (see page 26, Fig 2) and finishing at a corner. Insert the narrow Pink 150 ribbon. Make small bows from remaining ribbon and stitch at corners of quilt.

Spread the lining fabric wrong side up. Place the wadding on top. Lay the quilt on top, right side up. Pin the corners, then pin all round. Work a four-petalled Lazy Daisy at the corners of all the blocks, through all thicknesses. Work a French Knot in the centre of the daisy. Trim the lining fabric back to 12mm (½in) from the quilt edges, turn under and hand-sew to back of quilt.

Designed by Audrey Vincente Dean

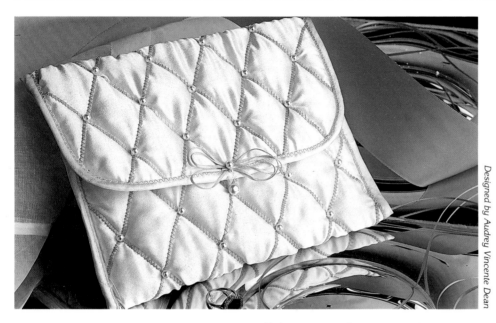

Designed by Audrey Vincente Dean

Quilted evening purse

English or wadded quilting consists of layers of fabric with wadding sandwiched between, stitched together in patterns to produce a raised effect. Traditionally, quilting stitchery is worked with running stitches or back stitches, but machine-stitching is often used in modern quilting.

Narrow ribbon looks pretty used for hand quilting in running stitches. Ribbon can also be used for machine quilting, as illustrated on the purse.

Materials required

Finished size 17×20cm (6¾×8in)
30×60cm *(12×24in)* good-quality satin fabric for quilting
30cm *(12in)* square of the same fabric for bias strip binding
30×60cm *(12×24in)* muslin
30×60cm *(12×24in)* polyester wadding
23×50cm *(9×20in)* lining fabric
4.40m *(4⅞yd)* of 1.5mm *(¹⁄₁₆in)*-wide Pink 150 polyester satin ribbon
54 small pearl beads, 1 larger pearl bead and 2 very small pearl beads
Matching Drima sewing threads
Pattern paper
Dressmakers' carbon pencil

Preparation

Draw out the paper pattern. Draw a rectangle 23×50cm *(9×20in)*. Round off the corners. Draw a line for the pocket fold 18cm *(7¼in)* from one end. Draw a line for the flap fold 18cm *(7¼in)* away. Mark each fold. This pattern includes 12mm *(½in)* seam allowance all round.

Prepare the satin fabric for quilting. Spread the fabric flat, right side up. Using a ruler and dressmakers' carbon pencil, draw a line diagonally from one corner to the other. Mark parallel lines each side, 3cm *(1¼in)* apart. Complete the diamond pattern by drawing lines on the opposite diagonal. Baste the satin, wrong side down, to wadding. Baste the muslin to the wadding. Cut the remaining satin fabric into bias strips 2.5cm *(1in)* wide.

Preparing the machine

Thread the sewing-machine with pink sewing thread. Fit the embroidery foot to the machine. From the front, thread the ribbon end down into the hole in the foot, under it and out at the back (Fig 1). You may find that a piece of fuse wire twisted into a loop helps to pull the ribbon through. Set the machine to a fairly wide zigzag stitch and to the width of the ribbon.

Working the quilting

Place the marked fabric right side up under the presser foot so that you are ready to work the longest diagonal line, which runs from corner to opposite corner. The ribbon end should lie just off the corner of the fabric, about 2.5cm *(1in)*.

Place your hands each side of the presser foot and stretch the fabric between them. As you stitch, the ribbon will be fed through under the zigzag stitching. Stitch right across the fabric, cut the ribbon end and threads and start the next line of quilting on the same edge of the fabric as before. Work all the quilting lines in the same direction.

Turn the fabric and work the other way to complete the diamond pattern. Pull all ribbon ends and threads to the wrong side. Tie off thread ends.

Use the paper pattern to mark the outline of the purse on the right side of the quilting. Work a row of machine stitches all round the shape, stitching 6mm *(¼in)* from the line to secure the ribbon ends. Cut away excess fabric.

Lining the purse

Use the paper pattern to cut out the lining. Place the quilted fabric and lining wrong sides together and baste. Machine-stitch together all round. Trim the seam allowance back to the inner line of stitches. Bind the edges of the purse with the bias strips. Stitch ribbon along the edges of the binding on the right side, using zigzag stitch and the same technique as for quilting.

Finishing

Sew pearls to the points of the diamonds all over the purse. Fold on the fold lines and hand-sew the side pocket seams. Make a stitched loop for fastening the purse and sew on a large pearl to correspond with the loop. Sew the two tiny pearls to the flap and make a bow under the pearls with remaining ribbon.

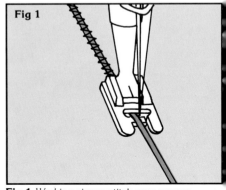

Fig 1 *Working zigzag stitch over narrow ribbon, using the embroidery foot*

Patchwork

Patchwork worked from pieces of ribbon is a way of using a wider range of colours and patterns than would be possible with conventional fabrics. Traditionally, patchwork using templates is worked by cutting backing papers for fabric patches, basting them together and then oversewing with tiny stitches. Ribbon will work on hexagons, octagons, squares and triangles, but not diamonds because they have narrow angles. Ribbon can also be used for machine patchwork.

Clamshell motif

The motifs on the dress and jacket illustrated are worked with polyester satin ribbons, using a technique that involves zigzag machine-stitching.

The three motifs use three clamshells in Light Pink 117, six clamshells in Light Orchid 430 and nine in Light Blue 305.

Materials required
45×25cm *(18×10in)* lightweight iron-on interfacing
57mm *(2¼in)*-wide single face polyester satin ribbons as follows:
25cm *(10in)* Light Pink 117; 50cm *(20in)* Light Orchid 430; 60cm *(24in)* Light Blue 305
Matching Drima sewing threads
Tracing paper, thin card

Preparation
With a cool iron, press the ribbons to the interfacing. Trace the clamshell (Fig 1) and draw the shape on to thin card. Cut out and use for a template.

Working the design
Trace round the card on ribbons so that you have three Light Pink 117 clamshells, six Light Orchid 430 and nine Light Blue 305. Space the clamshells 15mm *(⅝in)* apart. Cut out the clamshells with 3mm *(⅛in)* extra on the semi-circular edges.

Baste the clamshells to the ground fabric in the order shown in Fig 2. Set the sewing-machine to close zigzag stitch and to 3mm *(⅛in)* width. Machine-stitch all the clamshells on the semi-circular edges from dot to dot on the clamshell shape (Fig 1). Turn the 'stems' of the clamshells under, press and hand-sew.

Designed by Jennifer Banham

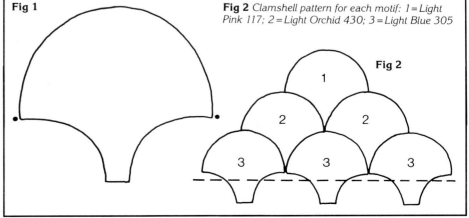

Fig 1

Fig 2 *Clamshell pattern for each motif: 1 = Light Pink 117; 2 = Light Orchid 430; 3 = Light Blue 305*

Fig 2
1
2　2
3　3　3

Ribbon Weaving

Ribbon weaving is one of the simplest of the needlecrafts – almost anyone of any age can master it. The tools required are minimal and patterns can be as simple – or as complex – as you like. It is the superb colours and textures of modern polyester ribbons that provide the excitement of this traditional craft.

Choosing ribbons

When choosing ribbons for weaving you should make sure they are colourfast, washable by hand or in a machine, non-shrink and crease-resistant. If you choose polyester ribbons to work with, you will be certain that you have the best quality for the craft.

Of the two satin types, single face and double face, single face is more suitable for weaving. Polyester grosgrains are now available in a vast range of colours and patterns, and there are washable velvet ribbons, Jacquards, Lurex ribbons and printed polyester satins, all of which add both texture and originality to a design.

Lace and broderie anglaise (eyelet) are often used with ribbons, and in weaving they add richness to the texture, with pretty results.

Tools and equipment

You need a flat, padded surface to work on. An ironing board or cork bathmat is ideal for small items, and for larger pieces of weaving pad a table top with a folded blanket. You will also need some glass-headed dressmakers' pins, a tape-measure, scissors, ruler, pencil and lightweight iron-on interfacing.

The basic technique

In the simplest terms, ribbons are pinned out on a padded surface and woven with the fingers, working over a piece of lightweight iron-on interfacing. Weaving can be worked from right to left, left to right or even bottom to top – whatever suits you. When weaving is finished, the ribbons are pressed on to the interfacing, bonding the ribbons into a fabric which can then be used to make all kinds of items, such as cushions, curtain ties, place mats, wall hangings and even small rugs, as well as a variety of fashion accessories.

Traditional ribbon weaving

Ribbon weaving is an old craft and was originally worked on a piece of lining fabric. Some crafts workers prefer this method when weaving for fashion garments, when a soft finish is required.

Cut the lining fabric to the desired shape and size, including seam allowances. Pin to a padded board. Cut, pin and weave ribbons as described overleaf, stages 4-9. To secure the weaving, baste round the outside edges of the work, stitching each ribbon end to the lining fabric and removing pins as you go. Machine-stitch all round in the seam allowance, before making up the mounted, ribbon-woven fabric.

All the cushions can be made from the weaving patterns given in this chapter. Instructions for making up cushions are on page 24

Designed by Christine Kingdom

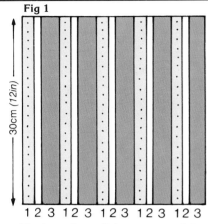

Fig 1

30cm (12in)

1 2 3 1 2 3 1 2 3 1 2 3 1 2 3 1 2 3

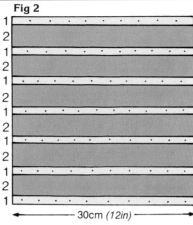

Fig 2

1
2
1
2
1
2
1
2
1
2
1
2
1
2
1

30cm (12in)

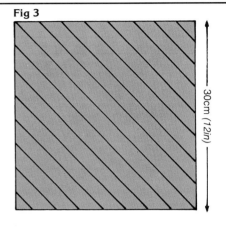

Fig 3

30cm (12in)

Estimating ribbon quantities

For the three simplest weaves (Plain, Patchwork and Zigzag, see overleaf) you will be working with a warp (the lengthwise ribbons) and a weft (the ribbons you weave with). Fig 1 shows how to measure ribbon quantities for a

30cm (12in) square in Plain weave, using three different widths of ribbon as warp. Fig 2 shows how to work out the quantities of two ribbons of different widths used as weft. Fig 3 shows how to estimate for diagonal weave.

When estimating ribbons for a project – whether it is a square, a circle, a heart shape or a garment pattern piece – draw similar diagrams life-size for yourself.

Figs 1 and **2** *From your diagrams calculate the quantity of each width of warp and weft ribbon separately*

Fig 3 *Measure the central diagonal and continue measuring ribbon lengths, working out to the corners*

Plain weave

Plain weave

A cushion cover finished size 30cm (12in) square in Plain weave is a good beginner's project.

1. Pencil a 30cm (12in) square on the wrong side (non-adhesive side) of lightweight iron-on interfacing and add 2.5cm (1in) all round for seam allowance. You now have a 35cm (14in) square.

2. Cut out the piece of interfacing and pin, adhesive side up, on a padded surface.

3. Calculate your ribbon quantities (see previous page). For the weave illustrated above 23mm (⅞in)-wide polyester satin ribbons in Peach 720 and White 029 were used.

4. Cut an odd number of warp ribbons into 35cm (14in) lengths. Start at the top left-hand corner of the square. Place the first ribbon with its cut edge on the edge of the interfacing and 2.5cm (1in) in from the left-hand edge (Fig 1). Pin the top end of the ribbon and leave the other end free.

5. Pin the next warp ribbon to the right, edges touching. Continue to pin ribbons for the warp, positioning the last ribbon 2.5cm (1in) in from the right-hand edge.

6. You can now begin weaving. Cut an odd number of weft ribbons into 35cm (14in) lengths.

7. Fix a safety pin to the end of the first weft ribbon. Weave it under, over, under alternate warp ribbons until the row is complete (Fig 2). Position the ribbon 2.5cm (1in) from the top edge of the interfacing and pin at both ends. It is advisable to angle the pins away from the work – you'll see why at the bonding stage.

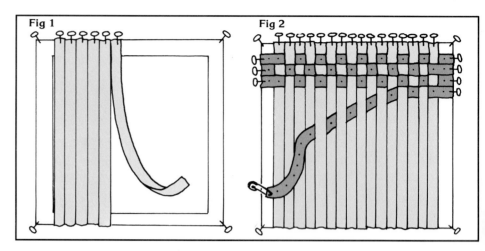

Fig 1 *The warp ribbons are pinned on the top edge only of the interfacing, starting and finishing 2.5cm (1in) from the side edges*

Fig 2 *The weft ribbons are then woven through the warp ribbons. The first weft ribbon is positioned 2.5cm (1in) from the top edge of the interfacing and pinned at both ends. The pins are angled away from the work so that the completed woven panel can be pressed easily*

8. With the next weft ribbon start by going over the first warp ribbon, then under, over and so on, to the end of the row. Push the weft ribbon up so that ribbon edges touch, and pin down both ends.

9. Continue weaving rows, in the order described in stages 7 and 8, until the interfacing is completely covered with woven ribbons. Pin the last weft ribbon, at the bottom of the square, 2.5cm (1in) from the bottom edge. Check to see that all the ribbons are straight and the edges touching. Pin the bottom ends of the warp ribbons.

Bonding the ribbons

Dry-press the ribbon weaving with an electric iron on 'wool' setting. As the pins are angled away from the work you should be able to press right up to the edges. The light pressing will be enough to fix the ribbons to the interfacing, and you can now remove the pins.

Turn the weaving over and steam-press the back of it (or use an ordinary, hot electric iron and a damp cloth). Let the weaving cool. The finished square of woven fabric is now ready to make up into a cushion cover (see page 24 for technique).

Patchwork weave

Patchwork weave

There are several patterning possibilities in this weave and it is one that shows ribbons of different textures to best effect. Ribbons of the same width are always used.

1. Working with three colours, as shown in the illustration above, pin an odd number of warp ribbons, colours A, B and C, in this order: A,B,A,C: A,B,A,C: and so on across.

2. The colour sequence for the weft ribbons is the same (A,B,A,C) but they are woven as follows:

Row 1: Under 1, *over 2, under 2, over 2, under 2, repeat from * to end.

Row 2: Under 1, over 1, under 1, over 1, repeat to end.

Row 3: Over 2, under 2, over 2, under 2, repeat to end.

Row 4: Over 1, *under 1, over 3, under 1, over 3, repeat from * to end.

Zigzag weave

Zigzag weave

This weave uses two colours and can be worked with ribbons either of the same width or different widths. The weave is worked horizontally and vertically, as shown in the illustration, or you can work diagonally, starting from a corner.

1. Pin down an odd number of warp ribbons, alternating colour A and colour B.
2. Weave weft ribbons, alternating colours A and B as follows:
Row 1: Over 2, under 2, over 2, under 2, to end.
Row 2: Under 1, *over 2, under 2, over 2, repeat from * to end.
Row 3: Under 2, over 2, under 2, over 2, to end.
Row 4: Over 1, *under 2, over 2, under 2, repeat from * to end.

Tumbling blocks weave

This has an interesting three-dimensional look and is called Tumbling Blocks after the needlework patchwork design that it resembles.

There are two stages to this weave. Ribbons in three colours are required, A, B, C, and in two different widths, as follows:

Colours A and B: same width, with Colour B darker than A.

Colour C: narrower width than A and B and the lightest tone.

1. Pin down an odd number of colour A warp ribbons.
2. Weave weft ribbon colour B as follows:
Row 1: Over, 1, *under 1, over 2,

Miniature weaving

Very narrow ribbons can be woven into a fabric to make small, pretty accessories. The basic technique is similar to that described for wider ribbons but the weaving is done using a blunt-ended needle instead of the fingers, and the warp ribbons are pinned down at both ends, to make the needle-weaving easier.

Miniature ribbon weaving can be used to make sachets and pincushions (as shown on the front cover), and colourful fashion accessories such as the buttons shown below. Weave

1.5mm *(¹/₁₆in)*-wide ribbons over lightweight iron-on interfacing, press as instructed on the opposite page and then use the resulting woven fabric to cover button moulds.

Designed by Ann Johnstone

under 1, over 2, repeat from * to end.
Row 2: Under 1, over 2, under 1, over 2, to end.
Row 3: Over 2, under 1, over 2, under 1, over 2, to end.
Repeat these three rows to cover the weaving area.
3. Work ribbon colour C diagonally. The length of each ribbon strip will be different, so weave from a long piece of ribbon and cut off each strip after it has been woven. Place the first ribbon at the top left corner and work to the bottom right corner, weaving as follows:
Over 1 weft (colour B), under 2 warp (colour A), over 2 weft, under 2 warp.

Continue to weave in this order, working to the left of the first diagonal ribbon, then to the right, until work is completed.

Tumbling Blocks weave, first stage

Tumbling Blocks weave, second stage

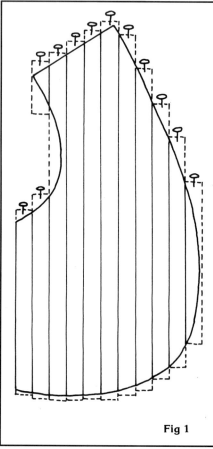

Fig 1

Fig 1 *The warp ribbons are pinned to the shape of the pattern piece but left untrimmed on the edges. The weft ribbons are also pinned untrimmed*

Fig 2 *Graph pattern for Candy-Coloured Bolero, 1sq=5cm (2in)*

Candy-coloured bolero

Once you have mastered the basic techniques of ribbon weaving squares, rectangles and circles, you can go on to weaving pieces of fabric for dressmaking.

The weaving process is exactly the same; the technique lies in cutting ribbons to different lengths to follow a pattern shape.

Weaving for dressmaking

For an entire garment, such as the bolero illustrated, choose patterns with simple outlines and without detailed seaming and darts. If you are working only part of a garment in weaving – a yoke, collar or cuffs perhaps – again, the pattern piece should be of a simple design, without complicated seaming.

When weaving for a garment, use the paper pattern to estimate the quantity of ribbons required. Having decided the width of ribbon you want, draw pencil lines vertically and horizontally across the pattern pieces to represent ribbon widths. Measure and total the ribbon quantities. Place the paper pattern pieces under lightweight iron-on interfacing laid adhesive side up. Trace all the pattern lines on to the interfacing.

Cut ribbons to fit the shape of the pattern pieces but when pinning them in position do not trim the ends to the precise outline (Fig 1). Work any of the weaves described on pages 48-49.

If you are weaving for small areas of decoration, such as collars, cuffs or the yoke of a baby gown, work a piece of weaving of sufficient length and depth, then pin the pattern piece to it and cut out exactly as for ordinary fabric.

Materials required

Measurements: bust 91cm (36in); length from shoulder 46cm (18in)
50cm (½yd) of 114cm (45in)-wide lining fabric
50cm (½yd) lightweight iron-on interfacing
50cm (20in) square fabric for bolero back (polyester, linen, satin, etc)
13mm (½in)-wide single face polyester satin ribbons as follows:
4.70m (5⅛yd) Mint 530 and Sherbet Pink 153; 4.40m (4⅞yd) Pale Lavender 413 and Peach 720; 4.25m (4⅝yd) Baby Maize 617; 4m (4½yd) Light Blue 305; 3.50m (3⅞yd) White 029
4.25m (4⅝yd) of 3mm (⅛in)-wide White 029 double face polyester satin ribbon
Squared pattern paper, 1sq=5cm (2in)

Preparation

Draw a paper pattern from the graph pattern (Fig 2). The pattern is for a garment that measures 91cm (36in) at the armhole level. As this is a loose-fitting garment, without fastenings, the bolero will also fit two smaller sizes. For larger sizes, you will need to buy a suitable commercial paper pattern and estimate ribbon quantities as described in Weaving for dressmaking.

Working the weaving

Cut two Fronts in iron-on interfacing and lay side by side for ribbon weaving to ensure that they match.

Pin the warp ribbons as follows: *Pale Lavender 413, Sherbet Pink 153, Mint 530, Pale Lavender 413, Peach 720, Light Blue 305, Baby Maize 617*. Repeat from * to *.

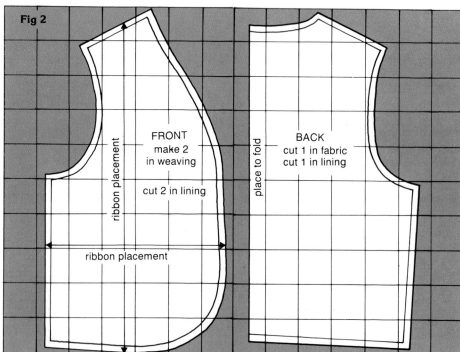

Fig 2

ribbon placement

FRONT
make 2
in weaving

cut 2 in lining

ribbon placement

place to fold

BACK
cut 1 in fabric
cut 1 in lining

The weft ribbons are woven in Plain weave as follows:
White 029, Sherbet Pink 153, Mint 530, Pale Lavender 413, Peach 720, Light Blue 305, Baby Maize 617. Repeat from * to *.

Making up the bolero

When the weaving is completed, fix the ribbons to the interfacing by pressing (see instructions on page 48). Trim to cutting lines. Work a line of machine-stitching in the seam allowance.

Using the paper pattern, cut the Fronts from doubled lining fabric. Cut one Back from lining fabric on the fold. Cut one Back from the polyester, linen or satin fabric on the fold.

Stitch ribbon-woven Fronts to fabric Back on side seams and shoulder seams.

Finishing

Press seams open. Stitch side seams and shoulder seams of lining. Pin the lining, right side to right side of fabric, to the bolero. Baste and then stitch round on Fronts, Back and armhole edges, leaving the seam open on Back hem for turning. Press seams flat, then turn the garment right side out and press edges again, easing the lining to the inside of the garment. Close the seam with hand-sewing.

Make a flat plait with the narrow White 029 double face polyester satin ribbon (see page 23, Fig 1) and hand-stitch all round garment edges.

Velvet and Lurex bolero

Using the same pattern, you can make yourself a glamorous evening bolero to wear with a long skirt.

Choose a jewel-toned velvet ribbon and weave it with Silver or Gold Lurex ribbons; for instance, Century Blue 353 velvet ribbon with Gold Lurex ribbon edged with matching Century Blue. Or try the effect of Silver Lurex ribbon edged with Red 250 mixed with velvet ribbons in Red 250 and Scarlet 260. The 10mm (⅜in) width in both velvet and Lurex ribbons would look effective. Estimate your required quantities as instructed in Weaving for dressmaking.

Offray Design Studio

Covered in ribbons

A wedding photograph album with a ribbon-woven cover would make an unusual and charming gift for a bride. Tiny dressmaker roses made from ribbons are stitched to the cover, and the picture frame is trimmed with similar roses. Instructions are not given for the frilled ring cushion illustrated. If you would like to make this, follow the weaving pattern for the album. The finished size of the woven cushion front is 30cm (12in) square.

Ribbon-woven photograph album

The instructions given here are for an album 28×23cm (11×9in). You can adapt the instructions to albums of different sizes by making a life-size paper pattern (Fig 1). To do this, measure the depth of the album from top to bottom edges and add 2.5cm (1in) to the measurement. Measure the width from front across the spine to the back and add 2.5cm (1in) to the measurement. For the pockets, allow two pieces of fabric the depth of the album by 16cm (6¼in) wide. Also, allow fabric for piping the album. By drawing in the woven panel on the front cover you will be able to estimate how much ribbon you need for weaving (see page 47).

Materials required

For an album 28×23cm (11×9in)
60cm (24in) of 114cm (45in)-wide white moiré taffeta fabric

1 piece of 30×54cm (12×21in) polyester wadding
2 pieces of 25×20cm (10×8in) polyester wadding
33×28cm (13×11in) lightweight iron-on interfacing
1.70m (1⅞yd) piping cord
97cm (38in) of 2.5cm (1in)-wide insert lace
For weaving: single face polyester satin ribbons as follows: 6.90m (7⅝yd) of 7mm (¼in)-wide Cream 815; 5m (5½yd) of 7mm (¼in)-wide Light Pink 117; 4.90m (5⅜yd) of 10mm (⅜in)-wide White 029; 2.30m (2½yd) of 7mm (¼in)-wide Sherbet Pink 153; 6.90m (7⅝yd) of 10mm (⅜in)-wide White 029 Feather-edge satin ribbon
For dressmaker roses: 60cm (24in) of 10mm (⅜in)-wide White 029, Cream 815, Sherbet Pink 153 single face polyester satin ribbons
For lace insertion: 97cm (38in) of 10mm (⅜in)-wide Cream 815 single face polyester satin ribbon
For streamers: 1m (1⅛yd) of 3mm (⅛in)-wide White 029 double face polyester satin ribbon

Preparation

Cut two pieces of taffeta 30×54cm (12×21in) for the outer cover and the lining. For the end pockets, which hold the cover in place, cut two pieces of taffeta 30×16cm (12×6¼in). Baste the large piece of wadding to the wrong side of one

Fig 1 *For a different-sized album measure and estimate fabric and ribbon quantities from a diagram drawn life-size on pattern paper*

Fig 2 *Place the lining over the piped cover piece, right sides facing, and baste round the edges*

taffeta piece for the cover. Cut and join 2.5cm (1in)-wide strips of taffeta to cover the piping cord.

Make two dressmaker roses (see pages 6-7) from each of the White 029, Cream 815 and Sherbet Pink 153 ribbons.

Lay the interfacing adhesive side up on a padded surface for ribbon weaving an area 33×28cm (13×11in)

Cut the warp ribbons into pieces 33cm (13in) long as follows: nine pieces Cream 815, nine pieces Light Pink 117, nine pieces White 029 Feather-edge and eight pieces White 029.

Cut the weft ribbons into pieces 28cm (11in) long as follows: eight pieces Sherbet Pink 153, eight pieces White 029, 14 pieces White 029 Feather-edge, 14 pieces Cream 815 and seven pieces Light Pink 117.

Working the weaving

Work in Plain weave (see page 48) as follows:
Warp: left to right, *Cream 815, Light Pink 117, White 029 Feather-edge, White 029*. Repeat from * to * ending with White 029 Feather-edge.
Weft: weave from top to bottom as follows: *Sherbet Pink 153, White 029, Cream 815, White 029 Feather-edge, Light Pink 117, Cream 815, White 029 Feather-edge*. Repeat from * to * ending with White 029.

Complete weaving and finish by pressing, as instructed on page 48.

Making up the cover

Baste the two smaller pieces of wadding to the wrong side of the ribbon weaving. Trim weaving level with the edges of the wadding. Wrap the padded taffeta cover round the

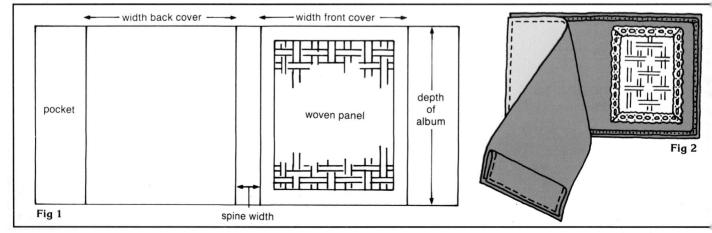

← width back cover →	← width front cover →
pocket	woven panel

Fig 1   spine width   depth of album

Fig 2

Fabric-covered picture frame

Make a frame like the one in the picture with this simple technique.

Materials required
Heavy cardboard as estimated
Fabric as estimated
Strong, all-purpose glue

Preparation
Measure the picture to be framed. Add 12.5cm (5in) to the depth measurement. Add 10cm (4in) to the width. Cut two pieces of card to these dimensions. Cut two pieces of fabric to same size plus 12mm (½in) all round. Cut a cardboard strut to the depth measurement by 7.5cm (3in). Cut a piece of fabric to this size. Cut a second piece of fabric 12mm (½in) larger all round.

Make a window in the front card piece by laying the picture on it, centring it on the width and 5cm (2in) from top edge. Pencil round. Cut out window 6mm (¼in) inside the line. Fold cardboard strut piece 5cm (2in) from top end.

Making the frame
Cover the cardboard pieces as follows. Lay fabric wrong side up. Centre frame back piece on top. Cut fabric corners off diagonally. Fold fabric on to card and glue down (Fig 1). Cover front frame piece in the same way. Cut away fabric from window leaving 12mm (½in) allowance. Snip into corners, fold fabric on to card and glue down (Fig 2). Glue frame front to back on sides and bottom edge (Fig 3). The picture slides in at the top.

Cover cardboard strut with larger fabric piece, folding and glueing down on the wrong side (see Fig 1). Glue smaller fabric piece on wrong side to cover card. Fold strut again and glue to frame back 5cm (2in) from top edge (Fig 4).

Fig 1

album. Pin the piece of weaving on the centre of the front cover. Remove cover and baste weaving in position. Machine zigzag stitch all round.

Thread Cream 815 ribbon through the insert lace. Baste and then stitch the lace around the ribbon-woven panel, starting and finishing at a corner. Make mitred corners (see page 26, Fig 2). Pin the prepared piping round the cover on the right side, matching raw edges and making round corners, as shown in the picture.

Lining and pockets
Fold the pocket pieces down the length of fabric, wrong sides

together. Baste the pockets to each end of the taffeta lining piece, on the right side. Baste the pockets in position. Place the lining piece over the piped cover piece with right sides facing and baste all round (Fig 2). Machine-stitch close to the piping, leaving a gap in the seam for turning.

Turn to the right side. Press and hand-sew the open seam.

Finishing
Sew the dressmaker roses to the top left corner of the album with narrow White ribbon in between, leaving 15cm (6in) streamers.

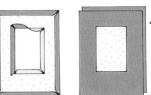

Fig 2   **Fig 3**   **Fig 4**

Ribbon Roses

Of all the flowers possible in flower-making crafts, the rose is the most popular.
All kinds of materials can be used to make roses, but lustrous polyester satin
ribbons produce the loveliest effects. Ribbon roses can be made on long stems
for vase arrangements or they can be used to make all kinds of floral accessories.
For parties and festive occasions, ribbon roses make charming room decorations,
displayed anywhere where fresh flowers might be used.

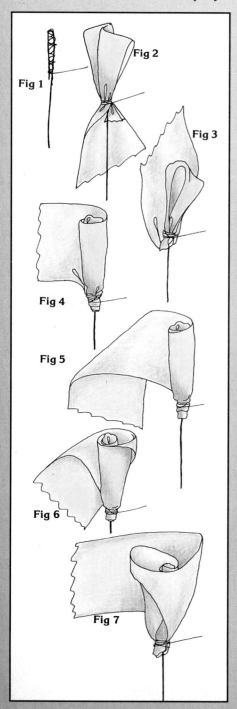

Fig 1
Fig 2
Fig 3
Fig 4
Fig 5
Fig 6
Fig 7

Estimating ribbon quantities

The width of the ribbon used
determines the size of the finished
rose. As a general guide, you need
about 1m *(1⅛yd)* of 39mm and
57mm *(1½in and 2¼in)*-wide ribbon
to make a full-petalled rose. When
using narrower ribbons, 16mm and
23mm *(⅝in and ⅞in)*, you need
about ¾ metre *(¾yd)*.

Materials required

Single face polyester satin ribbon
Stem wires, florists' binding wire,
    stem binding tape
Artificial rose leaves

Preparing the stem

Bend a loop on the end of the stem
wire. Thread the end of the binding
wire through the loop and wind
round to fasten (Fig 1).

Making the bud

Fold the ribbon end over the loop.
Gather it round the stem. Wind the
binding wire round tightly, *anticlockwise,* about three times (Fig 2).

  Now pull the ribbon up and out
sideways (Fig 3). Roll the bud on to
the ribbon to make a tight tube,
about four turns (Fig 4). Wind the
binding wire tightly round the
bottom of the tube, still anticlockwise.

First petal

Every petal is made in the same way
– on a diagonal fold in the ribbon.
The bud must always lie inside the
rose, so it should not be allowed to
come above the edge of the fold.

  Fold the ribbon end away from you
diagonally (Fig 5). Moving only your
right hand, turn the bud on to the
centre of the fold (Fig 6). Place your
left thumb over the bud so that you

can change your right-hand grip,
then continue turning the bud on to
the fold until the ribbon is straight
again. You have made a cone shape
of ribbon around the bud (Fig 7).

More petals

Make another diagonal fold in the
ribbon and turn the ribbon cone on
to the fold as before (Fig 8). Continue
turning until the ribbon lies straight
again (as in Fig 7). The binding wire
will twist itself around the base of the
rose as you work, so you will find it
easier if you pull the binding wire
tightly round the base of the rose
every time you make a petal.
Continue making petals until the
rose is the desired size.

Finishing the ribbon

Bring the ribbon end down to the
base of the rose and gather it
together with your fingers (Fig 9).
Grip the whole rose firmly in your
left hand and wind the binding wire
tightly round the base of the rose,
then take the wire down the stem for
about 2.5cm *(1in)*. The wire should
catch in all the ribbon edges to make
the rose secure on its stem.

Applying the stem binding tape

Stem binding tape becomes slightly
sticky when stretched. Lay the end of
the tape directly under the rose head
and press, stretching it slightly. Turn
the rose, pressing the tape over the
wire to cover it, then continue
covering the stem with tape (Fig 10).
About 2.5cm *(1in)* from the rose
head you can add the first leaf. Lay it
against the stem and bind in with the
stem. Add more rose leaves in the
same way.

Rosebuds

These are made from a square cut from wide ribbon, either 39mm or 57mm (1½in or 2¼in) depending on the size of the bud required.

Prepare the stem as for ribbon roses. Fold the square of ribbon in half diagonally (Fig 11), wrap it round the stem loop and bind tightly with wire round the base of the bud. Cover the wire and stem with binding tape.

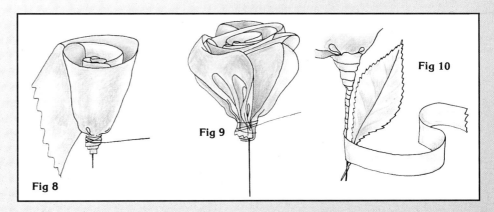

Fig 8

Fig 9

Fig 10

Fig 11

Designed by Pamela Woods

Wedding roses

Ribbons make beautiful weddings in so many ways — for the bride and her attendants, for the wedding cars, for the church or the room where the service is held, and at the reception itself, decorating the tables and the cake. Bridal flowers made from ribbons are a new idea and make a lasting memento of the day.

Flower ball

Materials required

Approximately 12.5cm *(5in)* diameter styrofoam ball
30 ribbon roses made from 23mm *(⅞in)*-wide Pink 150 single face polyester satin ribbon
30 ribbon roses made from 23mm *(⅞in)*-wide White 029 single face polyester satin ribbon
3m *(3¼yd)* of 7mm *(¼in)*-wide White 029 double face polyester satin ribbon
Stem wires, florists' binding wire, white stem binding tape

Preparation

Cover the rose stems with binding tape and cut into 5cm *(2in)* lengths. Make 10 loops with White ribbon (Fig 1), tape the wire stems and cut to 5cm *(2in)*.

Bend one end of a full-length stem wire into a loop. Push the straight end right through the ball so that the loop lies against the bottom of the ball. Make a small loop on top and snip off the excess wire.

Assembly

Press the Pink and White roses into the ball to cover it. Then press four of the ribbon loops into the ball, at intervals between the roses.

Push three ribbon loops into the top of the ball and three into the bottom. Cut the loops at the bottom diagonally. Cut two or three loops at the top. Tie two 30cm *(12in)* lengths of ribbon to the bottom hook and cover with binding tape. Tie the remaining ribbon to the top hook in a bow, with a handle to carry the ball. Cover the hook with tape.

Designed by Cathryn Brooker

Bride's flower tiara

This lovely head-dress is particularly suitable for long hair. It is worked on a stem wire from the centre outwards. The stem wire has hooked ends so that the tiara can be fastened into the hair with grips.

Materials required

6 ribbon roses made from 23mm *(⅞in)*-wide White 029 single face polyester satin ribbon
4 ribbon roses made from 10mm *(⅜in)*-wide White 029 single face polyester satin ribbon
4 small artificial white carnations
2 silk rose leaves
2 silk ivy leaves
Sprigs of artificial white heather
6 ribbon loops (see Fig 1) made from 3mm *(⅛in)*-wide White 029 double face polyester satin ribbon
Stem wires, florists' binding wire, brown or white stem binding tape

Preparation

Tape the roses just under the heads and leave the stems untaped. Prepare each of the carnations by pushing a thin stem wire through the seed pod and twisting the ends together to form a short stem.

Assembly

Cover a stem wire with binding tape and bend the ends into open hooks. Starting at the centre, bind three large roses to the stem wire with binding wire. Place a carnation to the right and left of the roses, then place sprigs of heather diagonally. Wire into position.

Add two ribbon loops diagonally either side of the centre roses and wire in place. Bind in rose leaves, ivy leaves, roses, ribbon loops, heather and carnations, tapering off the arrangement as you reach the ends of the stem wire base. The last pieces to be wired are two sprigs of heather at each end.

Bridesmaid's coronet

Bridesmaids of any age can wear a coronet of real or artificial flowers. Make coronets 15cm *(6in)* diameter for adult bridesmaids and about 12.5cm *(5in)* diameter for little girls.

Assembly

Real or artificial flowers are taped together with stem tape to form a long strip, and the ends are then bound into a circlet. The technique is

simple and can be used for ribbon roses mixed with artificial flowers, as shown in the picture.

Start with three flowers. Hold them at different levels and tape them together with stem tape. Position flowers, leaves and prepared ribbon loops (Fig 1) on the left and right of the centre flowers, and continue taping the stems together until you have reached the desired length for the coronet. Bring the last stems round to the beginning. Trim the ends and insert them between the flowers. Bind with tape. Finish the coronet with two lengths of ribbon tied at the back on the join, to make long streamers. Cut ribbon ends diagonally to prevent fraying.

Bride's bouquet

The bouquet uses a variety of white artificial flowers together with ribbon roses, which helps to give the bouquet a fragile appearance.

Materials required

6 rosebuds made from 57mm (2¼in)-wide White 029 single face polyester satin ribbon
5 medium-sized roses made from 23mm (⅞in)-wide White 029 single face polyester satin ribbon
11 small roses made from 10mm (⅜in)-wide White 029 single face polyester satin ribbon
8 large roses made from 39mm (1½in)-wide White 029 single face polyester satin ribbon
15 sprigs of artificial white heather
6 sprays of artificial lily of the valley
6 artificial stephanotis flowers
Silk ivy leaves, lily of the valley leaves
23mm (⅞in)-wide White 029 double face polyester satin ribbon for the handle and bow
Florists' binding wire, green stem binding tape

Preparation

All roses should be made with long stems. The other flowers and leaves, etc should also be wired on to long stem wires and finished with binding tape.

Assembly

The focal point of the bouquet should be the large roses in the centre. Group the large roses round a single large rose. Hold the stems near to the ends. Arrange the medium-sized roses round the outside, interspersing with heather

and lily of the valley. Position the green leaves towards the outer edge.

The stephanotis flowers, some of the heather and the very small roses should be used near the bottom of the bouquet, to form a 'pear shape'. Gently withdraw some of the flowers and move others back into the bouquet. Keep the outer edges 'light' using the smaller flowers and the sprigs of heather. Allow the flowers and sprays at the lower front to trail down. Bend some of the rose heads to point slightly upwards.

Still holding the stems together unbound, check the look of the bouquet in a mirror. Check the side views too — these are seen twice as much. When you are satisfied with the arrangement, bind the bouquet's stems with wire to form a handle. Bind White ribbon round the handle and finish with bows.

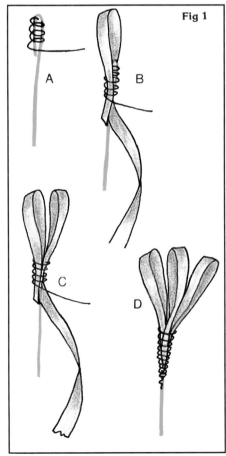

Fig 1 *Ribbon loops: bend a loop on the end of a thin stem wire and thread binding wire through (A). Fold ribbon into a loop and secure with binding wire (B). Make two more ribbon loops and secure in the same way (C) and (D). Cover binding wire and stem with binding tape*

Festive Ribbons

Ribbons provide colour, excitement, glamour, prettiness and nostalgic charm for every festive occasion. They are an essential ingredient in decorating the home, for party tables, for the Christmas tree and for tying gifts — and they add countless fashion touches to party clothes and accessories.

Ribbon rose table centre

This festive table centre is made from dried material, plastic ornaments and ribbon roses, made as described on pages 54-55.

Materials required

20cm *(8in)* diameter silver cake board
15cm *(6in)* diameter styrofoam ball
Clear adhesive
Gold-painted teazles, fir cones and dried rose hips
Sprigs of pine
3 red plastic apples, 1 candle
Stem wires, florists' binding wire
1.50m *(1⅝yd)* of 10mm *(⅜in)*-wide Silver Lurex ribbon
3 large roses made from 39mm *(1½in)*-wide Red 250 single face polyester satin ribbon on 15cm *(6in)* stems
5 medium-sized roses made from 23mm *(⅞in)*-wide Red 250 single face polyester satin ribbon on 15cm *(6in)* stems
4 small roses made from 16mm *(⅝in)*-wide Red 250 single face polyester satin ribbon on 15cm *(6in)* stems

Preparation

Push stem wires through the teazles, cones and rose hips and twist around pine sprigs. Twist ends to make stems. Slip a wire through each of the apples' hooks and twist ends to make a stem. Cut the Silver ribbon into six equal lengths and make each into a double bow with binding wire. Leave ends hanging. Twist ends of wire to make stems.

Assembly

Glue the ball to the cake board. Push pine into the ball all round. Mark the position of the candle in the ball. Cut a hole for it with a pointed knife. Arrange the gold-painted material, the apples and roses around the candle hole (see picture). Cut stem lengths as required for a decorative effect. Position Silver ribbon bows round the arrangement. Push the candle into its hole.

Ribbon wreath

Make this wreath for your front door or for an indoor wall decoration.

Materials required

30cm *(12in)* diameter styrofoam ring
Gold-painted fir cones and teazles
Red plastic apple, silver bauble
Small piece Oasis florists' block
Double face polyester satin ribbons as follows: 1.50m *(1⅝yd)* of 16mm *(⅝in)*-wide Red 250; 1.50m *(1⅝yd)* of 7mm *(¼in)*-wide Emerald 580; 2m *(2¼yd)* of 23mm *(⅞in)*-wide Emerald 580
1.40m *(1½yd)* of Red 250 Offray velvet tubing
1m *(1⅛yd)* of 10mm *(⅜in)*-wide Gold Lurex ribbon
Stem wires, florists' binding wire, adhesive tape

Preparation

Wind the wide Emerald ribbon round the ring and fasten ends with adhesive tape. Push stem wires through cones and teazles. Twist ends to make stems. Slip a wire through the apple's hook. Twist ends to make a stem.

Cut velvet tubing into eight equal lengths. Push a stem wire through each. Bend into loops and twist wires to make stems.

Cut the Red ribbon into six equal lengths and the Emerald ribbon into four equal lengths. Make multiple loops of each length with binding wire. Twist ends to make stems.

Cut the Gold Lurex ribbon into

three equal lengths. Wire into three multiple loops and twist ends to make stems. Wire the silver bauble and make a stem.

Assembly

Wire the florists' block to the back of the ring, on the ribbon join. Push the prepared material into the block, following the picture for the arrangement. Keep three Red velvet tubing loops, one multi-loop bow of Red ribbon and one fir cone for the top of the wreath.

Place five velvet loops at the back of the arrangement, then add the Red, Emerald and Gold multi-loop bows. Position the apple centre left and the teazles at the top, right and bottom centre. Arrange the bauble and fir cones as shown in the picture.

Wire the remaining velvet loops together for the top of the wreath. Wire the Red multi-loop bow to the top centre of the ring. Wire the fir cone to the middle of the bow. Wire in the velvet tubing loops, using one loop as the hanger.

Tubing dolls

Little ribbon dolls, made from velvet tubing and dressed in ribbons and felt, make charming Christmas decorations for the tree or for a party table. They also make amusing mascots to wear for school or club events. The basic doll is simple to make and takes only 20cm (8in) of velvet tubing.

Materials required

For one doll

20cm (8in) Offray velvet tubing
2 pipe cleaners
2.5cm (1in) diameter papier-mâché ball
4 beads for hands and feet, 1cm (³⁄₈in) diameter
All-purpose clear adhesive
Knitting yarn for hair
Flesh-coloured poster paint, black fibre-tipped pen for marking features

Preparation

Cut the velvet tubing as follows: one piece for arms 6.5cm (2½in) long; one piece for legs 8cm (3¼in) long; one piece for the body 5cm (2in) long. Cut two pieces of pipe cleaner, one for arms 8cm (3¼in) long and one for the body 8.5cm (3½in) long. From the second pipe cleaner, cut a piece for the legs 9.5cm (3¾in) long.

Push the pieces of pipe cleaner into the velvet tubing. Hold the tubing firmly so that the cotton core does not slip out.

Assembling the body

Bend the body piece in half. Lay the arms piece in between and glue in position. Hold with a pin (Fig 1A). Bend the legs piece in half. Spread a

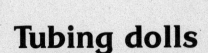

Fig 1

A

glue

B

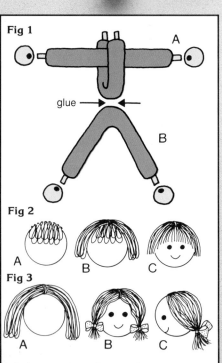

Fig 2

A   B   C

Fig 3

A   B   C

Designed by Valerie Janitch

ittle glue on the bend and then on he bend in the body piece. Leave for ive minutes, then press legs to body Fig 1B).

Trim a little pile from the pipe leaner ends. Spread with glue and ush on the hands and feet beads. he head is not put on to the body ntil after the doll is dressed.

lead and hair

aint the papier-mâché ball flesh- oloured. While it is drying, prepare he hair. For male character dolls, cut strip of card 7cm *(2¾in)* long. Vind knitting yarn round four or five imes. Slide the loops off and tie with piece of yarn about 2.5cm *(1in)* rom one end. Glue this to the top of he head, the short loops falling over he forehead (Fig 2A). Cut a second trip of card 8cm *(3¼in)* long and vind yarn round five times. Slide the oops off and tie the centre loosely.

Glue this on top of the head and to the sides (Fig 2B). When the glue is dry, cut the loops and trim the hair to the desired style (Fig 2C).

For female dolls, cut a strip of card 12.5cm *(5in)* long. Wind the yarn round five or six times, depending on how full the hair-style is to be. Slide the loops off and tie loosely in the centre. Glue the centre to the top of the head, then spread the loops to cover the sides of the head, glueing them in place (Fig 3A). Cut the loops. Two basic hair-styles are possible, side-bunched and tied back (Figs 3B and C).

Ringlets look pretty with a tied- back hair-style. Twist together very tightly six strands of yarn 8cm *(3¼in)* long. Make two ringlets and glue one each side of the head, falling over the ears. Draw the rest of the hair to the nape of the neck and tie.

Features

Dress the doll and glue on the head. Mark in the features with the black pen. These should be kept very simple — just a curved mouth and two round eyes. If a nose is indicated, it should be tiny. On character dolls use a tiny bead for a nose; glue or pin in place.

Dressing the dolls

You will see from the picture that the colour of the velvet tubing can often form part of the doll's clothing. The British policeman has a dark blue body, arms and legs, and the soldier has a red body and arms, with white legs to represent a uniform.

Felt has been used mostly for dressing the dolls illustrated. Ribbon is also a useful material for some items, such as the leprechaun's pointed hat and the Red Indian doll's dress, which is made from fringed striped ribbon.

Fairies and gnomes

Here are some more little dolls made with different kinds of ribbons. The sugar plum fairies have satin ribbon bodies filled with pot-pourri, while the gnomes have cardboard bodies covered with grosgrain ribbons and are wearing pointed ribbon hats.

Sugar plum fairies

Materials required

For one doll about 10cm (4in) tall
2.5cm (1in) diameter paper or pressed cotton ball, painted pink
Knitting yarn for hair
Pipe cleaner, cotton wool, glue
10cm (4in) narrow lace edging
15cm (6in) of 39mm (1½in)-wide single face polyester satin ribbon
25cm (10in) of 5mm (³⁄₁₆in)-wide Feather-edge double face polyester satin ribbon
25cm (10in) of 3mm (⅛in)-wide mini-dot double face polyester satin ribbon
30cm (12in) of 1.5mm (¹⁄₁₆in)-wide double face polyester satin ribbon
12.5×7cm (5×2¾in) piece of Offray craft ribbon for wings
Lavender or pot-pourri

Working the design

Cut the wide satin ribbon in two pieces. Sew the long edges together, right sides facing. Fold the tube lengthwise down the middle so that the seams are together. Sew up the bottom of the tube to make a bag. Turn to the right side. Hem the top edge and then gather with small running stitches. Drop in a little lavender or pot-pourri. Fill the bag with cotton wool.

Glue the pink-painted ball on to the pipe cleaner. Push the pipe cleaner down into the bag, making sure that the seams of the bag are at front and back. Pull up the gathering stitches to hold the head in position winding the thread ends round the 'neck'.

Glue lace, Feather-edge ribbon and mini-dot ribbon round the bottom of the bag, as shown in the picture. Glue Feather-edge ribbon down the centre front seam and mini-dot ribbon on top.

Designed by Valerie Janitch

Glue Feather-edge ribbon round the neck. Tie a knot in the centre of an 8cm (3¼in) length of narrow satin ribbon and glue at neck front.

Make hair from knitting yarn as described on page 61 and glue to the head. Glue a tiny bow of mini-dot ribbon at the front. Mark round dots for eyes and a tiny line for a nose with a black fibre-tipped pen.

Trace the wing shape (Fig 1). Cut a pair of wings from folded craft ribbon. Spread glue along the fold. Stick to the back body seam. Stitch a hanging loop of ribbon to the back of the body.

Christmas gnomes

Materials required

For one doll about 12.5cm (5in) tall
Thin card, cartridge paper, glue
8cm (3¼in) pipe cleaner
Table tennis ball, or paper ball, painted pink
Knitting yarn for hair and beard
Scraps of black felt
Red bead for nose
Small bell for hat
Sequin or silver button for buckle
70cm (28in) of 39mm (1½in)-wide grosgrain polka-dot ribbon
12.5cm (5in) of 7mm (¼in)-wide velvet ribbon

Working the design

Make the body as follows: cut a 3.5cm (1¼in) diameter hole in a piece of card. Roll up a piece of cartridge paper 4×25cm (1½ × 10in) and place inside the hole. Allow it to unroll and fit. Mark the join, remove the paper and glue into a tube. Glue a piece of polka-dot ribbon round the tube. Spread glue around top edge of the tube and press the ball on.

Glue velvet ribbon around the middle of the tube for a belt. Glue on the 'buckle'. Make hair with knitting yarn, as described on page 61, and glue to the head. Make the beard by laying a strand of yarn along a pencil, then winding more yarn round the pencil and over the strand for about 8cm (3¼in). Glue the ends of the strand back along the loops. Slip the loops from the pencil and glue round the gnome's chin. Glue the red bead on the face for a nose and mark two dots for eyes with a black fibre-tipped pen.

Trace the arm shape (Fig 2) and cut from folded cartridge paper. Cover both sides of the arms piece up to the wrists with polka-dot ribbon. Paint hands pink. Glue the arms to the back of the body and bend the hands to the front. Glue cartridge paper to the black felt and cut out two 2cm (¾in) circles for feet. Glue to the bottom edge of the tube.

Make the hat as follows: cut two pieces of polka-dot ribbon 17cm (6¾in) and 10cm (4in) long. Centre the short strip against the long strip,

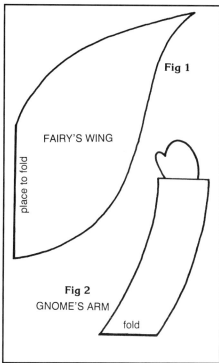

Fig 1 *Trace fairy's wing and cut from folded craft ribbon*

Fig 2 *Trace gnome's arm and cut from folded cartridge paper*

edges together, and oversew, right sides facing. Open out and press flat. Fold down the middle, right sides facing. Sew from the top of the fold diagonally to the corner through both thicknesses of ribbon. Trim off ribbon ends. Turn the hat to the right side and glue the pipe cleaner inside along the seam. This helps to keep the hat standing up. Sew the bell to the tip. Glue the hat to the head.

Ribboncraft tree trims

Nothing brings Christmas to life quite like dressing the tree. For every family, the tree is a special part of the tradition, with every ornament from another year bringing back memories. New additions will become part of that tradition. Here are some ideas for making tree trims from ribbon oddments for next Christmas and many Christmasses to come.

Balls and baubles

The Christmas balls illustrated are plain white satin decorated with pinned ribbons. Styrofoam balls can be trimmed in the same way.

All you need is a selection of narrow satin ribbons in brilliant colours, a few Lurex ribbons and some glass-headed dressmakers' pins, sequins and beads.

Slip beads and sequins on to the pins and push them into the balls to secure ribbons. That is all there is to it – plus some creativity! You can pleat, fold, loop and gather ribbons on to pins but leave some of the white ball showing for contrast. Hanging loops are made with a doubled length of ribbon secured into the top of the ball with a pin or hook.

Red and white ball *(top)* Red satin ribbons are secured into loops with pearl beads on pins. A tassel of red ribbons is secured to the bottom of the ball.

Zigzag ball *(left)* Lurex and satin ribbons are secured into zigzag patterns with sequins on pins.

Ball with bows *(centre)* Little bows made of 1.5mm *(1/16 in)*-wide ribbons are secured with beads on pins.

Banded ball Multi-coloured satin and Lurex ribbons are secured horizontally and vertically round the ball with pearl beads on pins.

Embroidered baubles The tree ornaments shown in the picture are 8cm *(3 1/4 in)* square and are made from plastic canvas straight-stitched with 1.5mm *(1/16 in)*-wide ribbons. They would be a good project for children learning to embroider. Use colourful satin ribbons and contrast with glittering Lurex ribbons. Keep the designs simple, working in geometric patterns across two, three and four threads of canvas. Back the baubles with red or green felt.

More ideas for Christmas trims

Velvet tubing makes charming tree trims. Cut 15cm *(6in)* lengths of red and green tubing and push a stem wire into each. Bend into shapes, such as bells, stars and leaves. Slip gold, silver or glass beads on to binding wire and wire a group of beads to each ornament. Suspend with a loop of narrow Lurex ribbon.

Narrow satin tubing ribbon is a versatile material for making decorations. Slip a thin stem wire or pipe cleaner into a 23cm *(9in)* length of tubing. Wind the tubing around a pencil to make a 'spring'. Wire a group of satin and Lurex springs together for a star ornament.

Ribbon stars Cut eight 15cm *(6in)* lengths of Lurex ribbon. Wind 15cm *(6in)* lengths of binding wire round the middle of each ribbon and twist the ends together to make a stem. Open out the ribbons flat. Hold the eight ribbons together and form into a star shape. Twist the stems together for a hanger. Fish-tail the ribbon ends.

Christmas rings Cover small brass or plastic rings with 1.5mm *(1/16 in)*-wide satin and Lurex ribbons worked in buttonhole stitch. Slip small glass or gold beads on to short lengths of binding wire and fasten to the inside top of the rings.

Rosettes Gather a 20cm *(8in)* length of 12mm *(1/2in)*-wide lace into a rosette. Make two or three dressmaker roses (see pages 6-7) with 23mm *(7/8in)*-wide red, pink or pale blue ribbon. Stitch roses to the centre of the rosette with loops of narrow Gold or Silver Lurex ribbons. Stitch a ribbon loop at the back for hanging the rosette.

Offray Design Studio